INTELLECTUAL PROPERTY IN THE 21ST CENTURY

PATENT LITIGATION REFORM: PROPOSALS AND PERSPECTIVES

INTELLECTUAL PROPERTY IN THE 21ST CENTURY

Additional books in this series can be found on Nova's website under the Series tab.

Additional e-books in this series can be found on Nova's website under the e-book tab.

INTELLECTUAL PROPERTY IN THE 21ST CENTURY

PATENT LITIGATION REFORM: PROPOSALS AND PERSPECTIVES

RICHARD K. GUTIERREZ
EDITOR

nova publishers
New York

NOTICE TO THE READER

Library of Congress Cataloging-in-Publication Data

ISBN: 978-1-63485-526-6

Published by Nova Science Publishers, Inc. † New York

CONTENTS

PREFACE

Congress has shown significant interest in altering the current patent system in response to concerns about entities that engage in patent litigation tactics that have been criticized as abusive or deceptive. Many congressional hearings on the topic of patent litigation abuse have been held in the 114th and 113th Congresses, and several legislative proposals have been introduced; one bill in the 113th Congress, H.R. 3309, the Innovation Act, was passed by the House in December 2013. In June 2015, the House Judiciary Committee approved the Innovation Act (H.R. 9) by a vote of 24 to 8, and the Senate Judiciary Committee passed the PATENT Act (S. 1137) by a vote of 16 to 4; both bills are awaiting floor action. This book describes how the major provisions of current patent litigation reform legislation, with a particular focus on these two bills that have seen the most legislative activity, would change existing patent law to address the perceived problems in the patent litigation system.

In: Patent Litigation Reform
Editor: Richard K. Gutierrez

ISBN: 978-1-63485-526-6

Chapter 1

PATENT LITIGATION REFORM LEGISLATION IN THE 114TH CONGRESS*

Brian T. Yeh and Emily M. Lanza

SUMMARY

This report describes how current patent litigation reform legislation would change existing patent law to address the perceived problems caused by entities that engage in patent litigation tactics that have been criticized as abusive or deceptive. The bills introduced in the 114th Congress include the Innovation Act (H.R. 9), Protecting American Talent and Entrepreneurship Act (PATENT) Act (S. 1137), Demand Letter Transparency Act of 2015 (H.R. 1896), Targeting Rogue and Opaque Letters (TROL) Act (H.R. 2045), and the Support Technology and Research for Our Nation's Growth (STRONG) Patents Act of 2015 (S. 632). The legislation includes the following changes to the patent system:

Heightened Pleading Requirements: The Innovation Act and the PATENT Act would require parties alleging patent infringement in a civil action to include in the court pleadings specified details concerning each claim of each patent infringed, and the acts of the alleged infringer.

---

* This is an edited, reformatted and augmented version of a Congressional Research Service publication R43979, prepared for Members and Committees of Congress dated February 8, 2016.

Limits on Discovery: The Innovation Act (as reported by the House Judiciary Committee) and the PATENT Act propose limitations on discovery pending the resolution of certain motions, including motions to dismiss, transfer venue, and drop parties.

Transparency of Patent Ownership: The Innovation Act and the PATENT Act would require plaintiffs in patent cases to disclose to the United States Patent and Trademark Office (USPTO), the court, and all adverse parties information relating to entities that own or have a financial interest in the patent.

Customer-Suit Exception: The Innovation Act and the PATENT Act would allow a court to stay litigation against a customer of a product that contains allegedly infringing technologies, if the manufacturer of the product is a party to the same or other action on the same patent and other requirements are satisfied.

Shifting of Attorney Fees: The Innovation Act would require a district court to award attorney fees to a prevailing party in patent cases, unless the court finds that the nonprevailing party's position and conduct "were reasonably justified in law and fact or that special circumstances ... make an award unjust." The PATENT Act would require the prevailing party to make a motion to the court to determine whether the nonprevailing party's position and conduct were "objectively reasonable"; if they were not, then the court must award reasonable attorney fees to the prevailing party unless there are special circumstances that would make an award unjust.

Fee Recovery: The Innovation Act and the PATENT Act contain provisions that address the situation when the nonprevailing party alleging infringement is unable to pay the fee award and other expenses. The Innovation Act (as reported) and the PATENT Act would allow a defendant to submit a statement early in the litigation claiming that the plaintiff's primary business is the assertion and enforcement of patents; the plaintiff would then need to certify that it has sufficient funds to satisfy any potential award of attorney fees that may be assessed, and to identify (and provide notice to) any "interested parties" that could be held accountable for the award if the plaintiffs are unable to pay it.

Demand Letters: Several bills propose various approaches to address demand letters. The STRONG Patents Act and the TROL Act would impose specific enforcement and content requirements for demand letters. The Innovation Act expresses the sense of Congress that purposely evasive demand letters are abusing the patent system in a manner contrary to public policy. The Demand Letter Transparency Act proposes both disclosure and content requirements directed towards "abusive" demand letter practices, and the PATENT Act focuses on pre-suit notifications.

Post-Grant Review Reforms: The Innovation Act, PATENT Act (as reported by the Senate Judiciary Committee), and the STRONG Patents Act would mandate that the Patent Trial and Appeal Board (PTAB), in inter partes review (IPR) and post-grant review (PGR) proceedings, follow the same claim construction standard used by district courts. The Innovation Act and the PATENT Act (as reported) would require the PTAB to consider prior claim construction by a court in a civil action in which the patent owner was a party. In addition, the Innovation Act and the PATENT Act would narrow the estoppel effect arising from a PGR. The Innovation Act (as reported) and the STRONG Patents Act would heighten the standing requirements for persons wanting to initiate a PGR or IPR. The STRONG Patents Act would also require the IPR/PGR petitioner to prove unpatentability of a patent claim by "clear and convincing evidence."

Elimination of USPTO Fee Diversion: The STRONG Patents Act would permit the USPTO to spend all fee revenue that it collects without further appropriation action or fiscal year limitation.

Venue: The Innovation Act (as reported) would impose limitations on the judicial districts in which a civil action may be brought for patent infringement or for a declaratory judgment that a patent is invalid or not infringed.

Assistance for Small Businesses: The Innovation Act, STRONG Patents Act, and the PATENT Act contain provisions designed to help small businesses that participate in the patent system either as patent owners or as defendants.

INTRODUCTION[1]

Congress has shown significant interest in altering the current patent system in response to concerns about entities that engage in patent litigation tactics that have been criticized as abusive or deceptive. Many congressional hearings on the topic of patent litigation abuse have been held in the 114th and 113th Congresses,[2] and several legislative proposals have been introduced;[3] one bill in the 113th Congress, H.R. 3309, the Innovation Act, was passed by the House in December 2013. In June 2015, the House Judiciary Committee approved the Innovation Act (H.R. 9) by a vote of 24 to 8, and the Senate Judiciary Committee passed the PATENT Act (S. 1137) by a vote of 16 to 4; both bills are awaiting floor action.[4] This report describes how the major provisions of current patent litigation reform legislation, with a particular focus on these two bills that have seen the most legislative activity, would change existing patent law to address the perceived problems in the patent litigation system.

BACKGROUND

Patent Law Fundamentals

According to Section 101 of the Patent Act, one who "invents or discovers any new and useful process, machine, manufacture, or any composition of matter, or any new and useful improvement thereof, may obtain a patent therefore, subject to the conditions and requirements of this title."[5] Thus, in order for an invention to qualify for patent protection, it must fall within one of the four statutory categories of patent-eligible subject matter: processes, machines, manufactures, and compositions of matter. However, the U.S. Supreme Court has articulated certain limits to Section 101 of the Patent Act, stating that "laws of nature, natural phenomena, and abstract ideas" may not be patented.[6]

The U.S. Patent and Trademark Office (USPTO) issues a patent to an inventor after USPTO examiners approve the submitted patent application for an allegedly new invention.[7] An application for a patent consists of two primary parts: (1) a "specification," which is a written description of the invention enabling those skilled in the art to practice the invention, and (2) one or more claims that define the scope of the subject matter which the applicant regards as his invention.[8] Therefore, these claims define the scope of the patentee's rights under the patent.[9]

Before a patent may be granted, the USPTO examiners must find that the new invention satisfies several substantive requirements that are set forth in the Patent Act.[10] For example, one of the statutory requirements for patentability of an invention is "novelty."[11] For an invention to be considered "novel," the subject matter must be different than, and not be wholly "anticipated" by, the so-called "prior art," or public domain materials such as publications and other patents. Another statutory requirement is that the subject matter of an alleged invention must be "nonobvious" at the time of its creation. A patent claim is invalid if "the differences between the subject matter sought to be patented and the prior art[12] are such that the subject matter as a whole would have been obvious at the time the invention was made to a person having ordinary skill in the art to which said subject matter pertains."[13] Finally, the invention must also be "useful," which means that the invention provides a "significant and presently available," "well-defined and particular benefit to the public."[14]

The Patent Act grants patent holders the exclusive right to exclude others from making, using, offering for sale, or selling their patented invention throughout the United States, or importing the invention into the United States.[15] Whoever performs any one of these five acts during the term of the invention's patent, without the patent holder's authorization, is liable for infringement.[16] A patent holder may file a civil action against an alleged infringer in order to enjoin him from further infringing acts (by securing an injunction, also referred to as injunctive relief).[17] The patent statute also provides federal courts with discretion to award damages to the patent holder thatare "adequate to compensate for the infringement, but in no event less than a reasonable royalty for the use made of the invention by the infringer."[18] The usual term of patent protection is 20 years from the date the patent application is filed.[19] At the end of that period, others may use the invention without regard to the expired patent.

Because the Patent Act expressly provides that "patents shall have the attributes of personal property,"[20] patent holders may sell their patent rights in a legal transfer called an "assignment."[21] Alternatively, patent holders may grant others a "license" to exercise one of the five statutory patent rights.[22] A license is not a transfer of ownership of the patent, but rather is the patent holder's permission to another entity to use the invention in a limited way, typically in exchange for periodic royalty payments during the term of the patent.[23] A patent holder may grant to a licensee the right to practice the invention through a contract (typically known as a patent licensing agreement). The terms of the licensing agreement, however, may include conditions upon the grant of rights—for example, restricting the licensee from making the invention but allowing that party to sell it.[24] A licensee that performs an act that exceeds the scope of the license (through a violation of the limitations and conditions of the grant of rights) or refuses to comply with the terms of the license agreement (such as by refusing to pay the required royalties) is potentially liable to the patent holder for breach of contract as well as for patent infringement.[25]

The U.S. Court of Appeals for the Federal Circuit (Federal Circuit) is a specialized tribunal established by Congress that has exclusive appellate jurisdiction in patent cases.[26] Parties dissatisfied with the Federal Circuit's rulings may petition the U.S. Supreme Court to review the appellate court's decision. However, the Supreme Court is not required to entertain the appeal; it has discretion to decide whether to grant certiorari to review the case.[27]

Besides seeking legal relief for infringement in the federal courts, U.S. patent holders may also obtain an order from the U.S. International Trade Commission (ITC or Commission) preventing the importation of foreign goods that infringe their rights. The ITC is an independent, nonpartisan, quasi-judicial federal government agency responsible for investigating and arbitrating complaints of violations of Section 337 of the Tariff Act of 1930 (19 U.S.C. §1337), which prohibits unfair methods of competition or other unfair acts in the importation of products into the United States. Section 337 also prohibits the importation of articles that infringe valid U.S. patents, copyrights, processes, trademarks, or protected design rights. (The majority of unfair competition acts asserted under Section 337 involve allegations of patent infringement.)[28] The ITC has the power to order several forms of prospective injunctive relief, including ordering the U.S. Customs and Border Protection (CBP) to stop imports from entering U.S. borders (an exclusion order), or issuing cease and desist orders that prohibit parties from distributing or selling infringing articles from existing U.S. inventory. However, unlike the federal courts, the ITC lacks the statutory authority to award monetary damages for patent infringement (past or future).

Although issued patents are presumed to be valid, accused infringers may assert in court that a patent is invalid or unenforceable on a number of grounds.[29] The accused infringer could raise this argument as an affirmative defense or counterclaim when sued for patent infringement. A party could also preemptively file a "declaratory judgment action"[30] against a patent owner to challenge a patent's validity, if there is a case or controversy between them.[31]

However, the constitutionally based "case or controversy" requirement for federal judicial proceedings significantly limits the ability of members of the public to challenge the USPTO's decision to grant a patent. Unless the patent holder becomes involved in an actual, continuing controversy with another person, that person cannot successfully request that a court determine whether the patent is valid or not. To address this perceived deficiency, Congress established several administrative procedures that are conducted by the USPTO's Patent Trial and Appeal Board, or PTAB,[32] through which any interested person may challenge the validity of an issued patent. Three trial proceedings comprise the current system of administrative patent challenges: inter partes review (IPR), post-grant review (PGR), and the transitional post-grant review for covered business method patents (CBM). The three proceedings have different rules, timing, and eligibility requirements.[33] The proceedings may result in the confirmation of patentability of the original claims, an amended patent with narrower claims, or a declaration of patent invalidity.[34] A party dissatisfied with the PTAB's final written decision in an IPR, PGR, or CBM review may appeal directly to the Federal Circuit.

Patent Assertion Entities[35]

"Patent assertion entities" are people or companies that do not develop, manufacture, or sell any product covered by the patents they own. The business model of a patent assertion entity (PAE) instead focuses on buying and asserting patents against companies that have already begun using and developing the patent, often without knowledge of the PAE's ownership of the patent.[36] PAEs emerged alongside the burgeoning tech industry around the turn of the 21st century and gained notoriety with lawsuits claiming exclusive ownership of such ubiquitous technologies as wireless email, digital video streaming, and the interactive web.[37] The vast majority of lawsuits brought by PAEs end in settlements because litigation is risky, costly, and disruptive for defendants, and PAEs often offer to settle for amounts well below litigation costs to make the business decision to settle an obvious one.[38] PAEs are frequently referred to as "patent trolls," after the villains of folklore known to lie in wait under bridges they did not build, then emerge from the smog to demand tolls from unsuspecting travelers.[39] The term "troll" is controversial because it is both pejorative and ambiguous, often used imprecisely for any opportunistic or unpopular patent holder.[40] Instead, PAEs describe themselves as critical intermediaries. Some claim to offer "department stores" for patents, providing one-stop shopping for licensing and purchase.[41] Others suggest they serve key functions by enabling individual inventors to earn returns despite lacking the resources to enforce or commercialize their patents themselves.[42]

However, while PAEs may be considered a type of "non-practicing entity" (NPE), other NPEs can serve similar intermediary functions without engaging in "trolling" tactics.[43] PAEs are alleged to be one-of-a-kind in that they are said to speculate on patents—they bet on how much more a patent will be worth in the future, when it is asserted, and focus on high-risk high-yield acquisitions.[44] The Federal Trade Commission has explained that while other

NPEs transfer technologies that they or their clients invented and developed so that licensees can benefit from not having to develop them in-house, PAEs transfer nothing but a legal right not to be sued for using a technology that the licensee may have already invested in developing on its own, without help from the PAE or its patents.[45] PAEs also diverge from other NPEs that *enforce* patents because they focus on acquiring patents outright and asserting them on their own behalf, as opposed to providing services and collecting fees or a slice of the litigation award.[46]

Critics of PAEs argue that they extort the patent system through litigation by extracting licensing fees or damage awards from companies that cannot afford the cost of litigation. Critics also argue that "patent trolling" deters innovation and discourages companies from seeking patents, and thus delivering new products to the market.[47] According to the White House:

> PAE activities hurt firms of all sizes. Although many significant settlements are from large companies, the majority of PAE suits target small and inventor-driven companies. In addition, PAEs are increasingly targeting end users of products, including many small businesses.[48]

However, defenders of PAEs argue that they actually promote invention by increasing the liquidity and managing the risk of investments in applied research and invention, as well as by compensating small inventors.[49] By enlivening a secondary[50] market for patents, PAEs provide an exit option and/or extra revenue stream for a variety of patentees. They absorb and manage the high risk by spreading it across large portfolios of patents and extracting value out of otherwise low-value or dormant patents. Patentees who do not or cannot commercialize in the "primary" market for technology[51] might recoup their costs and perhaps see some returns by selling their patents to PAEs and retaining a cut of future royalties. PAEs suggest this function is especially essential for small inventors and NPEs that would otherwise have a hard time getting any value from their inventions.

LEGISLATION IN THE 114TH CONGRESS

The remainder of this report discusses and analyzes the key provisions of legislative proposals that have been introduced in the 114th Congress related to patent litigation abuse. The subject matter of the patent law reforms is presented below in no particular order.

Heightened Pleading Requirements

The U.S. Supreme Court recently adopted a rule, which went into effect on December 1, 2015, that abolished Federal Rules of Civil Procedure's Form 18.[52] According to Form 18, a complaint for patent infringement[53] needed to include four statements that assert jurisdiction, patent ownership, patent infringement by the defendant, and a demand for relief.[54] Plaintiffs typically relied upon the Federal Rules of Civil Procedure's Form 18 to structure their patent infringement complaint. Generally, the Federal Circuit had applied the "notice pleading standard" to patent infringement pleadings for the purpose of a motion to dismiss for failure to state a claim (a typical method by which a defendant may attempt to have a case dismissed at the beginning of the case). Under this standard, a court finds that the patent pleading statements contain sufficient particularity to survive a motion to dismiss for failure to state a claim if they notify parties of the general issues of the case. In *K-Tech Telecommunications v. Time Warner Cable,* the Federal Circuit held that the information required by the Federal Rules of Civil Procedure's Form 18 is sufficient for pleading a patent infringement claim as the form states a plausible claim and places the alleged infringer on notice.[55] Additionally, the Federal Circuit in *McZeal v. Sprint Nextel Corporation* found that a party does not need to describe the relationship between each element of the claim and the infringing device in a patent infringement complaint.[56] According to the court, specific information such as this "is something to be determined through discovery."[57]

Under the Supreme Court's recent changes to the federal rules, patent plaintiffs may no longer rely on the standard outlined in Form 18 but will likely need to comply with the higher pleading standard under *Ashcroft v. Iqbal*[58] and *Bell Atlantic Corp. v. Twombly.*[59] In *Twombly* and *Iqbal,* the Supreme Court established that federal courts must evaluate the "plausibility of claims" made at the pleading stage when determining whether a civil complaint should survive a motion to dismiss for failure to state a claim.[60] Therefore, under the *Twombly/Iqbal* standard, a complaint must contain enough factual allegations to state a claim that is plausible on its face. However, prior to the Supreme Court's recent changes, courts have generally found that *Iqbal* and *Twombly* do not apply to patent litigation pleadings because of Form 18 and its inherent notice pleading standard. The Federal Circuit held in the 2012 case *In re Bill of Lading Transmission and Processing System Patent Litigation* that a patent plaintiff needs only to follow the requirements in Form 18 to survive a motion to dismiss for failure to state a claim.[61] The court stated that "to the extent the parties argue that *Twombly* and its progeny conflict with the Forms and create different pleadings requirements, the Forms control."[62] Without Form 18, however, patent plaintiffs will likely need to conform their patent pleadings to the higher *Twombly/Iqbal* standard.

The Innovation Act, H.R. 9, proposes additional heightened initial pleading requirements for an infringement claim, as compared to the current requirements under the Federal Rules of Civil Procedure's Form 18. Under these new requirements, a party alleging infringement in a complaint must include specific details regarding the following:

- each patent allegedly infringed;
- all claims necessary to produce the identification of each process, machine, manufacture, or composition of matter ("accused instrumentality") that is alleged to infringe any claim of each patent identified above;[63]
- for each accused instrumentality alleged to infringe a claim, an identification with particularity (if known) of the name or model number of each accused instrumentality or a description of each accused instrumentality;
- for each accused instrumentality, a clear and concise statement of how it infringes each claim of each patent;
- for each claim of indirect infringement, the acts of the alleged indirect infringer that contribute to, or are inducing, a direct infringement;
- the authority of the party alleging infringement to assert each patent and the grounds for the court's jurisdiction; and
- each complaint filed that asserts any of the same patents[64]

Like the Innovation Act, the Senate's PATENT Act also proposes heightened pleading requirements, including such details as

- the identification of each patent allegedly infringed;
- the identification of each claim of each patent that is allegedly infringed;
- the identification (including the name, model number, or description) of the accused instrumentality that has allegedly infringed the patent;
- a description of how the accused instrumentality is allegedly infringing specific elements of the claim; and

- a description of the acts of the alleged infringer that allegedly contributed to or induced the direct infringement, for claims of indirect infringement.[65]

The PATENT Act would not require such details in the initial pleading as the authority of the party alleging infringement to assert each patent and the principal business of the party alleging infringement, as outlined in the House's Innovation Act. Instead, the Senate bill would require the patentee to disclose specific information to the court and each adverse party no later than 14 days after the filing of the pleading.[66] These disclosure requirements would cover the identity of the patent assignee(s), the right to enforce the patent at issue, any ultimate parent entity, and entities that would have a particular financial interest in the patent at issue.[67] Both the Innovation Act and PATENT Act would also explicitly eliminate the Federal Rules of Civil Procedure's Form 18.[68]

Both the PATENT Act and the Innovation Act provide that if the information is not readily accessible, then the party may generally describe the information with an explanation of why such undisclosed information was not readily accessible.[69] Similarly, both bills also exempt from the proposed heightened pleading requirements any civil action that includes a claim for relief arising under Section 271(e)(2) of the current Patent Act relating to certain drug claims.[70]Commentators have linked "patent trolls" together with the current patent pleading requirements for a patent infringement claim.[71] They have argued that the minimal information required in a patent infringement complaint encourages PAEs to initiate "frivolous" lawsuits that otherwise would not survive the initial pleading state under a more stringent standard. Proponents of these pleadings changes state that such heightened pleading requirements would force a plaintiff to consider the alleged infringement instrumentality more carefully and decide whether infringement has occurred before filing the suit.[72] Supporters of heightened pleading requirements also argue that "not providing the necessary information at the beginning of a case in the complaint slows down the litigation and makes it inefficient and expensive for both parties."[73] Additionally, these proponents assert that heightened pleadings standards would not impose a greater burden on the plaintiff, who would develop a good-faith case, and providing such information at the early stages of litigation would improve efficiency and costs.[74] However, some commentators believe that the heightened pleading requirements would render patent enforcement impractical. According to these opponents, the plaintiff may not have the information available at this stage of litigation, as the discovery process typically reveals the information necessary to build a successful infringement claim.[75]

Limits on Discovery and Cost-Shifting

The Federal Rules of Civil Procedure permit discovery[76] into any unprivileged matter that is relevant to the claim or defense of any party.[77] This broad definition leads to costly discovery in patent litigation.[78] During the discovery process, the court may decide to hold a "Markman hearing,"[79] during which a judge examines evidence concerning the parties' disputes over the meaning and language of a patent claim that defines the boundaries of the invention. (Also referred to as "claim construction," or the interpretation of a patent's claims, this process largely determines the scope of the patent owner's proprietary rights.) For these hearings, courts must consider volumes of evidence produced during discovery relating to many different aspects of claim construction including evidence regarding the definition, meaning, scope, and pertinent art of the claim.[80]

The Innovation Act (as reported) would postpone discovery if the defendant makes a motion to sever a claim or drop a party for misjoinder; (2) transfer the action to another venue; or (3) dismiss the action.[81] Such motion must be filed within 90 days after service of the complaint and must include a declaration or other evidence in support of the motion. There are four exceptions to this stay of discovery provision:

1. the court may allow such discovery that the court deems is necessary to decide the motion to sever, drop a party, dismiss, or transfer the action;
2. the provision does not apply to an action in which the patent holder seeks a preliminary injunction to prevent harm arising from the manufacture, use, sale, or importation of an allegedly infringing product that competes with a product made or sold by the patent holder;
3. parties may consent to voluntary exclusion from these proposed limitations on discovery; and
4. the provision does not apply to any civil action that includes a claim for relief arising under 35 U.S.C. Section 271(e)(2) relating to certain drug claims.[82]

Like the Innovation Act (as reported), the Senate's PATENT Act would require a court to stay discovery pending the resolution of preliminary motions (which must be filed prior to the first responsive pleading), including the motion to dismiss, the motion to transfer venue, and the motion to sever accused infringers.[83] The bill would provide a court with the discretion to allow limited discovery to resolve these motions or a motion for a preliminary injunction or to preserve evidence or otherwise prevent specific prejudice to a party, if the court would find that additional discovery is necessary.[84] Similar to the Innovation Act, the PATENT Act would also grant parties with the opportunity to exclude themselves voluntarily from these proposed limitations.

Supporters of these proposed limitations on discovery note that the technical nature and complexity of patent litigation inherently leads to the extensive document discovery, and correspondingly encourages frequent settlements to avoid this high cost.[85] These supporters have stated that the propensity towards settlements in patent litigation encourages PAEs to file infringement suits. Critics of these discovery limitations have raised concerns that the discovery limitation provision may cause "patent litigation in the overwhelming majority of patent cases [to] incur significant across-the-board delays and increased expense for all parties."[86] Others have argued that the discovery stay provision could be subject to abuse; for example, a "defendant could ... invoke a stay of discovery by moving to transfer venue or to sever, even though the merits of a venue or severance motion have no bearing whatsoever on whether or not the plaintiff will ultimately be allowed discovery."[87]

Transparency of Patent Ownership[88]

Under current law, within a month after the filing of a civil action involving a patent, the clerks of the federal courts must provide written notice of the action to the USPTO director that describes the names and addresses of the parties, the name of the inventor, and the number of the patent upon which the action is based.[89] The USPTO director is then required to enter this information in the file of that patent.

Section 4 of the Innovation Act would amend this section of the Patent Act to impose specific disclosure requirements upon plaintiffs upon the filing of an initial complaint for patent infringement. (Similar to the exemption for the new pleading requirements, the Innovation Act's patent ownership disclosure requirement would not apply to any civil action that includes a cause of action for patent infringement under 35 U.S.C. §271(e)(2).)[90] Upon the filing of an initial complaint for patent infringement, plaintiffs would be required to disclose to the USPTO, the court, and all adverse parties the following information relating to entities that own or have a financial interest in the patent:

1. the assignee(s) of the patent(s) involved in the case;
2. any entity with a right to sublicense or enforce the patent(s) at issue;
3. any entity, other than the plaintiff, that the plaintiff knows to have a financial interest[91] in the patent(s) at issue or in the plaintiff;
4. the ultimate parent entity[92] of any assignee, or the entities identified in #2 and #3 above;
5. a clear and concise description of the principal business, if any, of the party alleging infringement;[93]
6. a list of each complaint filed, of which the party alleging infringement has knowledge, that asserts or asserted any of the patents identified above;[94]
7. for each patent identified, a statement as to whether the patent is subject to certain licensing requirements (imposed by the federal government, a foreign government, or by a standards development organization).[95]

Section 4 of the Innovation Act would require the plaintiff to notify the USPTO of any changes in the identity of the assignee of the patent or the entities described above, within 90 days of such change.[96] Failure to comply with this ongoing duty of disclosure would result in the plaintiff being barred from recovering either enhanced damages or reasonable fees and other expenses incurred in connection with the infringement lawsuit (with respect to infringing activities occurring during the period of noncompliance), "unless the denial of such damages or fees would be manifestly unjust."[97] In addition, the Innovation Act directs a court to award to a prevailing party accused of infringement any reasonable fees and other expenses that the party incurred to uncover the updated information about the assignee or entities, "unless such sanctions would be unjust."[98]

Section 4 of the Innovation Act grants the USPTO director the power to issue regulations to establish a registration fee in order to recover the cost of administering the "disclosure of interests" requirement, which includes the costs to facilitate collection and maintenance of the information submitted by plaintiffs and "to ensure the timely disclosure of such information to the public."[99]

According to the sponsors of the Innovation Act, the amendments made by Section 4 "will ensure that patent trolls cannot hide behind a web of shell companies to avoid accountability for bringing frivolous litigation."[100] However, a critic of this provision argued that it would be "needlessly burdensome" and that the required disclosure "could lead to the revelation of confidential financial and licensing agreements";[101] furthermore, he noted that if such information is relevant to the litigation, "it is readily discoverable under current rules, with appropriate protective orders to maintain needed confidentiality."[102]

The PATENT Act would require similar initial disclosures by a patentee in a patent infringement lawsuit as the Innovation Act.[103] Within 14 days of the patentee filing the pleading, the patentee would be required to notify the court and each adverse party of the following information:

1. The identity of each:
   a. assignee of the patent(s) at issue, and any "ultimate parent entity"[104] thereof;
   b. entity with a right to sublicense to unaffiliated entities or to enforce the patent(s) at issue, and any ultimate parent entity thereof;
   c. any other entity that the patentee knows to have a financial interest[105] in the patent(s) at issue, or in the patentee (and any ultimate parent entity thereof); and
2. For each patent that the patentee alleges to be infringed:
   a. a list of other complaints filed by the patentee in the three years before the filing of the action, as well as any other complaints filed in the United States (not by the patentee but that the patentee was aware of) that asserted the patent during the same three-year period;
   b. a statement as to whether the patent is subject to certain licensing requirements (imposed by the federal government or by a standards development organization).[106]

The PATENT Act would allow the patentee to file such information under seal if the patentee considers the information to be confidential (such as the home addresses of any individuals);[107] the Innovation Act does not contain a similar provision.

Within a month of the disclosure of the information listed above, the patentee would be required to file the information described in #1 above with the USPTO.[108] However, unlike the Innovation Act, the PATENT Act does not appear to place upon the patentee an ongoing duty of disclosure of such information to the USPTO.

In addition, Section 10 of the PATENT Act would require that an assignment of all substantial rights in any issued patent (and the name of the assignee and the ultimate parent entity of the assignee) be recorded in the USPTO within the following time periods:

1. no later than the date on which the patent is issued; and
2. when any subsequent assignment is made that results in a change to the ultimate parent entity
   a. no later than three months after such assignment is made; or,
   b. in the case of an assignment made as part of a corporate acquisition, not later than six months after the closing date of such acquisition.[109]

The PATENT Act provides similar consequences as the Innovation Act for failure to comply with the duty to disclose this information to the USPTO: that is, the party asserting infringement of a patent would be denied the right to receive either enhanced damages or reasonable fees and other expenses incurred in connection with the infringement lawsuit (with respect to infringing activities occurring during the period of noncompliance).[110] Like the Innovation Act, the PATENT Act would also require a court to award to a prevailing accused infringer reasonable attorney fees and expenses incurred to discover the identity of any undisclosed entity that was required to be disclosed.[111] Under the PATENT Act, the USPTO Director would be given the same authority granted by the Innovation Act to establish fees to administer the process of collecting and maintaining the submitted assignment information.[112]

Stays of Litigation Brought against Infringing Customers

Under the Patent Act, anyone who "makes, ***uses***, offers to sell, or sells any patented invention"[113] is potentially liable for patent infringement if such actions occur without the authority of the patent holder. Thus, the patent holder has the right to bring a lawsuit against not only the manufacturer or seller of products that incorporate allegedly infringing components, but also the customers who purchase and use those products.[114] Over the past few years, businesses (including restaurants, retailers, and grocery stores) and individuals increasingly have faced charges of patent infringement for their use of certain equipment that contain technologies such as Wi Fi, PDF scanning, email, and vehicle tracking.[115] A witness at a congressional hearing in 2013 described the situation as follows:

> Another patent litigation practice that has been sharply criticized is the institution of suits against large numbers of assemblers, distributors or retailers rather than the original manufacturer or provider of the component or product alleged to infringe. This tactic takes advantage of the fact that such suits threaten defendants with the disruption of aspects of their businesses that are at best tangentially related to the invention which is the subject of the patent, and that each individual defendant has less motivation to litigate the issue to final conclusion than the manufacturer of the product at issue. The result can be to collect enormous sums as the result of a very large number of small settlements whose cumulative value far exceeds the amount that could have been recovered from the original manufacturer.[116]

The judicially created response to such customer lawsuits is the so-called "customer suit exception" doctrine, which allows courts to prioritize litigation against or brought by the manufacturer of infringing goods over a lawsuit by the patent owner against customers of the manufacturer in the interest of efficiency and judicial economy.[117] The doctrine permits a court to stay an earlier-filed action against a customer involving an infringement product pending the outcome of a later-filed declaratory judgment action brought by the manufacturer of the accused product. As explained by the First Circuit Court of Appeals (prior to the creation of the Federal Circuit), "At the root of the preference for a manufacturer's declaratory judgment action is the recognition that, in reality, the manufacturer is the true defendant in the customer suit.... [I]t is a simple fact of life that a manufacturer must protect its customers, either as a matter of contract, or good business, or in order to avoid the damaging impact of an adverse ruling against its products."[118] However, the doctrine "has long existed in a state of relative disuse" and the Federal Circuit has affirmed its application in only one case in the last three decades.[119]

Section 5 of the Innovation Act would codify a modified version of the customer suit exception by amending the Patent Act[120] to require a court to suspend or postpone litigation against a customer of a product or process that contains allegedly infringing technologies, if several requirements are satisfied:[121]

1. the manufacturer is a party to the civil action or a separate action involving the same patent(s);
2. the customer agrees to be bound by the decisions of the court in the action involving the manufacturer, with respect to any issues that the customer and manufacturer have in common; and
3. the customer requests the court to stay the action no later than the later of (a) 120 days after the date on which the first pleading in the action is served (if such pleading specifically identifies the product or process that is the source of the customer's alleged infringement of the patent, and the pleading specifically explains how the product or process is alleged to infringe the patent), or (b) the date on which the first scheduling order in the case is entered.

The Innovation Act provides two limited exceptions to the manufacturer and customer's entitlement to a stay: (1) if the action involving the manufacturer will not resolve a major issue in the suit against the customer; or (2) if the stay unreasonably prejudices and would be manifestly unjust to the party seeking to lift the stay.[122] In addition, like the exemption for the new pleading and patent ownership disclosure requirements, the Innovation Act exempts from the customer suit stay provision any action that includes a cause of action for patent infringement under 35 U.S.C. Section 271(e)(2).[123]

Though the stay provision would only postpone, and not terminate, a cause of action against the customer, supporters of the stay provision assert that "in the vast majority of cases, a suit involving the manufacturer will eliminate all potential infringement liability of the customer."[124]

The Innovation Act (as reported) contains definitions of "covered customer," "retailer," and "end user" that limit the applicable scope of the customer stay provision, as follows:

1. A "covered customer" is a retailer or end user who is accused of patent infringement based on sale or use of a product/process alleged to infringe a patent, if the retailer or end user did not materially modify such product/process for their own purposes.
2. An "end user" is a user of a product/process alleged to infringe a patent and also an affiliate of such an end user, but does not include

an entity that manufactures (or causes the manufacture of) the product/process.

3. A "retailer" is an entity that generates its revenues mostly through sale of consumer goods or services, or an affiliate of such an entity, but does not include an entity that manufactures (or causes the manufacture of) the product/process alleged to infringe a patent.

The PATENT Act includes a customer stay provision similar to that of the Innovation Act (as reported).[125]

Both the Innovation Act (as reported) and the PATENT Act would require the written consent of the manufacturer to obtain a stay of an action against a customer only if the manufacturer had been made a party to the action on motion by the customer.[126] The PATENT Act contains the same provisions as the Innovation Act pertaining to situations in which a stay may be lifted: if the action involving the manufacturer will not resolve major issues in the suit against the customer, or the stay unreasonably prejudices or is manifestly unjust to the party seeking to lift the stay.[127] Also like the Innovation Act, the PATENT Act would exempt from the customer suit stay provision any action that includes a cause of action for patent infringement under 35 U.S.C. Section 271(e)(2).[128]

Shifting of Attorney Fees

For many years, patent cases were subject to the "American Rule," under which "[e]ach litigant pays his own attorney fees, win or lose."[129] Then in 1947, Congress enacted a fee-shifting provision that gave district courts the power to award attorney fees to the prevailing party in patent suits. The 1952 revision of the patent laws codified this provision at 35 U.S.C. Section This section of the Patent Act provides a court with the discretion to award "reasonable" attorney fees to the prevailing party (plaintiff or defendant) only "in exceptional cases."

However, the Federal Circuit in its 2005 opinion, *Brooks Furniture Manufacturing, Inc. v. Dutailier International, Inc.*,[130] established that courts may find an "exceptional case" under Section 285 in only two limited circumstances: (A) "when there has been some material inappropriate conduct" (during the litigation or in obtaining the patent from the USPTO) or (B) when the litigation is both (1) brought in subjective bad faith and (2) objectively baseless. In addition, *Brooks Furniture* held that the prevailing party must prove its entitlement to attorney fees by "clear and convincing evidence."[131] In part due to this strict standard, federal judges have rarely award these fees.[132]

In April 2014, the Supreme Court in *Octane Fitness v. Icon Health and Fitness* unanimously overruled the Federal Circuit's *Brooks Furniture* standard because the two-prong test "is unduly rigid, and it impermissibly encumbers the statutory grant of discretion to district courts."[133] Instead, the Court adopted a more lenient standard, holding "that an 'exceptional' case is simply one that stands out from others with respect to the substantive strength of a party's litigating position (considering both the governing law and the facts of the case) or the unreasonable manner in which the case was litigated."[134] The Court explained that district courts must make the Section 285 determination by considering the "totality of the circumstances."[135] The Court also rejected the Federal Circuit's requirement that prevailing parties establish their entitlement to legal fees by "clear and convincing evidence" and instead embraced a "preponderance of the evidence" standard.[136] In a companion case decided the same day as *Octane Fitness*, the SupremeCourt in *Highmark v. Allcare Health Management*[137] rejected the Federal Circuit's position that a district court's "exceptional case" determination is to be reviewed on appeal "de novo" and "without deference." Instead, the Court held that the district court's Section 285 determination must be reviewed on appeal under an abuse-of-discretion standard.[138]

By overruling the Federal Circuit's restrictive interpretation of Section 285, *Octane Fitness* and *Highmark* provide district courts with greater discretion in deciding whether to award fees, thus likely increasing the number of patent cases in which attorney fees are shifted. Thus, in evaluating whether to award attorney fees, a court must first assess whether the case is "exceptional" in accordance with the standard announced in *Octane Fitness,* and if so, the court may (or may not) choose to award the fees. It is unclear the extent to which these recent Supreme Court decisions will impact the filing of patent infringement lawsuits by patent assertion entities, yet supporters of patent litigation reform express hope that the increased prospect of paying the other party's litigation expenses could be a significant financial disincentive to PAEs' litigation tactics.[139] However, some observers predict that *Octane Fitness* and *Highmark* will not have a significant impact on PAEs because fee-shifting will remain limited:

> [R]ecent Supreme Court cases ... make clear that a case is exceptional only if it is unusually weak. Moreover, because district courts

> now have substantial discretion to decide whether to award fees, district courts that signal a reluctance to shift fees will invariably attract greater proportions of future patent lawsuits from plaintiffs eager to avoid any risk of fee-shifting. Finally, even when a court does shift fees to a plaintiff, the shell-corporation structure of many abusive litigants precludes any meaningful recovery for the defendant. So long as the entity that owns the patent rights holds no other assets, patent plaintiffs can effectively render themselves judgment proof.[140]

Section 3(b) of the Innovation Act would amend Section 285 to require a court, in any patent case, to award attorney fees to a prevailing party (plaintiff or defendant), *unless* the court finds that either

1. the nonprevailing party's position and conduct are "reasonably justified in law and fact"[141] or
2. there are "special circumstances (such as severe economic hardship to a named inventor) [that] make an award unjust."[142]

Although not explicitly stated by the legislation, the nonprevailing party would appear to have the burden of demonstrating the existence of either of these exceptions in order to rebut the presumption of an award of attorney fees. Supporters of the Innovation Act's fee-shifting provision believe that "allowing more liberal shifting of attorney fees against losing parties would reduce the frequency of such nuisance settlements, and would allow more defendants to challenge patents that are invalid or that have been asserted beyond what their claims reasonably allow."[143] On the other hand, those wary of fee-shifting provisions are concerned that they may benefit wealthy corporate parties to the disadvantage of individual inventors. They assert that "[a] 'loser pays' provision will deter patent holders from pursuing meritorious patent infringement claims and protects institutional defendants with enormous resources who can use the risk of fee-shifting to force inventors into accepting unfair settlements or dismissing their legitimate claims."[144]

The Support Technology and Research for Our Nation's Growth (STRONG) Patents Act of 2015 (S. 632) does not include a fee-shifting provision; instead, Section 101 of S. 632 (the "findings" section) asserts that the Supreme Court's *Octane Fitness* and *Highmark* rulings "significantly reduced the burden on an alleged infringer to recover attorney fees from the patent owner, and increased the incidence of fees shifted to the losing party."[145]

Section 7(a) of the PATENT Act expresses a "sense of Congress that, in patent cases, reasonable attorney fees should be paid by a nonprevailing party whose litigation position or conduct is not objectively reasonable."[146] Unlike the Innovation Act's creation of what appears to be a presumption of an award of attorney fees, Section 7(b) of the PATENT Act would require the prevailing party to first make a motion for the fees, after which the court must determine whether the position of the nonprevailing party was "objectively reasonable in law and fact, and whether the conduct of the nonprevailing party was objectively reasonable." If the court finds that the nonprevailing party's position and conduct does not satisfy these standards, the court must award reasonable attorney fees to the prevailing party, unless special circumstances would make an award unjust.[147] On June 4, 2015, the Senate Judiciary Committee approved two additions to the PATENT Act's fee-shifting provision:[148]

1. An explicit statement that "[t]he prevailing party shall bear the burden of demonstrating that the prevailing party is entitled to an award."
2. Examples of what constitutes a "special circumstance()... that would make an award unjust:" such as undue economic hardship to either—
    a. a named inventor (the same party cited by the Innovation Act) or
    b. an institution of higher education (as defined in section 101(a) of the Higher Education Act of 1965 (20 U.S.C. §1001(a)) (a party not listed in the Innovation Act's comparable fee-shifting provision)

Some practitioners believe that the Innovation Act's fee-shifting provision "would likely require fee awards in more cases than" the PATENT Act's comparable provision.[149]

Unlike the Innovation Act, the PATENT Act would exempt from the fee-shifting provision any action that includes a cause of action for patent infringement under 35 U.S.C. Section 271(e)(2).[150]

Recovery of Fee Awards from Interested Parties

The Federal Rules of Civil Procedure outline when a person must and may join as a party in litigation. Under Rule 19, a person must join as a party if, in the person's absence, the court would be unable to accord complete relief among existing parties, the person is unable to protect an interest, or a present party would be subject to a substantial risk of incurring multiple obligations.[151] Under Rule 20, a person may join as a plaintiff if all the plaintiffs could claim a right to relief for injuries arising from the same occurrence or transaction.[152] Likewise, persons may be joined as defendants if any right to relief is asserted against them jointly, severally, or in the alternative with respect to or arising out of the same transaction or occurrence.[153] The Patent Act outlines mores specific joinder requirements for a patent civil action. Under the Patent Act, a party may join a patent civil action as a defendant (accused infringer) only if any right to relief is asserted against the parties jointly and severally,[154] or arises out of the same transaction relating to the making, using, importing into the United States, offering for sale, or selling of the same accused product/process.[155] All defendants in the action must share the same questions of fact for joinder to occur.[156] Joinder cannot occur if "based solely on allegations that they each have infringed the patent or patents in suit."[157]

Section 3(c) of the Innovation Act would establish mandatory joinder rules when the nonprevailing party alleging infringement is unable to pay the fee award ordered by the court and other expenses. Thus, this provision would require a court presiding over a patent case to grant a defendant's motion to join an "interested party," "if such defending party shows that the plaintiff has no substantial interest[158] in the patent or patents at issue other than asserting such patent claim in litigation."[159] An "interested party" subject to this joinder provision would include a party that is a patent assignee, has a right to enforce or sublicense the patent, or has a direct financial interest in the patent, such as the right to any part of a damage award or licensing revenue.[160] The bill would exclude from the definition of an "interested party"

1. the plaintiff's employees;[161]
2. legal counsel retained on a contingency fee basis; or
3. an individual "whose sole financial interest in the patent or patents at issue is ownership of an equity interest in the party alleging infringement, unless such person also has the right or ability to direct or control the civil action." ("[M]embership on the board of directors alone is not sufficient to demonstrate such right or ability.")[162]

The Innovation Act (as reported) would create a statutory exception to the applicability of the joinder of interested parties provision for technology transfer organizations whose primary purpose is to facilitate the commercialization of technologies developed by one or more institutions of higher education, if such technology transfer organization is alleging infringement on behalf of an entity that is exempted from the joinder provision.[163]

In order for the joinder provision to apply to a patent infringement action, the Innovation Act (as reported) would require the defendant to file an initial statement (no later than 14 days before a scheduling conference is to be held or a scheduling order is due) expressing the good faith belief that the party alleging infringement has no substantial interest in the subject matter at issue other than asserting the patent in litigation.[164] Within 45 days of being served with such an initial statement, the plaintiff would then be required to file a certification that

1. the party will have sufficient funds to pay for any potential award of reasonable attorney fees;
2. the party has substantial interest in the subject matter at issue other than asserting the patent in litigation; or
3. there are no other interested parties.[165]

The Innovation Act would grant the court with the *discretion* to deny a motion to join if the interested party is not subject to service of process, or if the joinder would deprive the court of subject matter jurisdiction or render the venue improper.[166] The Innovation Act would *require* a court to deny a motion to join an interested party if the party did not receive "timely notice" of being identified as an interested party.[167] (The Innovation Act defines "timely notice" to mean actual notice, provided within 30 days after the expiration of when the plaintiff's certification (described above) is required to be filed, that the party has been identified in the plaintiff's initial disclosure regarding entities that have financial interests in the patent and which may be liable for paying an award of fees if the plaintiff is unable to pay it.[168])

A court would also be required to deny a motion to join an interested party if the interested party, within 30 days after receiving the notice described above, renounces in writing and with notice to the court and parties to the action, any ownership, right, or direct financial interest in the patent at issue.[169]

The Innovation Act would provide a court with discretionary authority to make an "interested party" who was joined under Section 3(c) of the act liable for any part of the award of attorney fees that the nonprevailing party is unable to pay.[170]

Mandatory joinder provisions, including that proposed by the Innovation Act, respond to the alleged lack of transparency regarding PAEs or the absence of financial resources held by some PAEs and their corresponding inability to pay fees to a prevailing defendant. Proponents of this proposed provision state that mandatory joinder would encourage greater transparency by granting patent defendants with further knowledge regarding all the parties who may have an interest in the litigation beyond the PAE "shell company."[171] Proponents of the joinder provision also argue that such a change would allow prevailing defendants to seek a greater financial award against PAEs, who may not have extensive financial resources, by permitting the defendants to seek financial recovery against additional parties.[172] Opponents of this provision argue that the mandatory joinder of third parties is "one-sided" and may restrict the ability of patent owners to enforce their patents.[173] Some have stated that joinder provisions such as the one proposed by the Innovation Act may harm business relationships that arise through licensing by forcing parties to join in order to pay damages and other fees.[174] Opponents also contend that joinder in this context for the purposes of fee-shifting raises constitutional concerns as the provision would create standing for parties that would otherwise not have standing.[175] Specifically, the opponents point to the scenario where "a defendant may join [as] a third-party at the end of the case for the purposes of fee-shifting, but the third-party had no standing to assert or defend themselves during the course of the legal proceedings."[176]

The PATENT Act contains a mechanism for recovering fee awards from interested parties that is similar to the Innovation Act (as reported). First, the PATENT Act's recovery of award provision would allow the defendant to file (no later than 14 days before a scheduling conference is to be held or a scheduling order is due) an initial statement expressing the good faith belief that the primary business of the plaintiff is the assertion and enforcement of patents (or the licensing that results from it).[177] Within 45 days of being served with such an initial statement, the plaintiff would then be required to file a certification that[178]

1. the party will have sufficient funds to pay for any potential award of reasonable attorney fees;
2. the party's primary business is not the assertion and enforcement of patents (or the licensing that results from it);
3. the identity of "interested parties," if any; or
4. it has no such interested parties.

The PATENT Act defines "interested party" for purposes of this section concerning the recovery of fees, to mean a person who has a substantial financial interest related to the proceeds from any settlement, license, or damages award resulting from the enforcement of the patent in the action.[179] However, the term does NOT include any of the following:[180]

1. an attorney or law firm providing legal representation in the action if the sole basis for its financial interest in the action arises from compensation related to the provision of legal representation;
2. a person who has assigned all right, title, and interest in a patent, except for passive receipt of income to an institution of higher education or a nonprofit technology transfer organization affiliated with the institution;
3. a person who would otherwise meet the definition of an interested party but whose financial interest is based solely on an equity or security interest that had been initially established when the party alleging infringement's primary business was not the assertion and enforcement of patents (or the licensing resulting from it); and
4. an insured depository institution whose sole basis for the financial interest arises from a loan or other debt obligation.[181]

The PATENT Act would place an ongoing duty on the plaintiff to update its certification within 30 days after a material change to any of the information provided within it.[182]Prior to filing the certification, the plaintiff must provide each identified interested party "actual notice in writing by service of notice in any district where the interested party may be found," in order to establish jurisdiction over the interested party for the sole purpose of enforcing an award of attorney fees, "consistent with the Constitution of the United States."[183] The notice must identify the action, the parties, the patents at issue, and the interest qualifying the party to be an interested party. The notice must also inform the recipient that the recipient may be held accountable for any award of attorney fees (or a portion thereof) resulting from the action in the event the plaintiff cannot satisfy the full amount of such award, unless the recipient submits a statement to the court and parties in the action, within 120 days of receiving the notice, that renounces its interest related to the enforcement of the patent.[184] The PATENT Act would make any interested parties who are timely served with this notice potentially liable to pay any attorney fees, or portion thereof, awarded by the court, in the event that the party alleging infringement cannot satisfy the full amount of the award.[185] However, interested parties would not be accountable if "a true and correct certification" is filed with the court that the plaintiff will have sufficient funds to pay for any potential award of reasonable attorney fees, or that the party's primary business is not the assertion and enforcement of patents (or the licensing that results from it).[186]

The PATENT Act grants an interested party the right to intervene in the action for purposes of contesting its identification as an interested party or its liability for attorney fees.[187] A court may, in the interest of justice, exempt from award recovery any party identified as an interested party. Finally, the PATENT Act would create a statutory exception to the applicability of the award recovery provision for any institution of higher education (as defined in 20 U.S.C. §1001(a), or under equivalent laws in foreign jurisdictions), or a non-profit technology transfer organization whose primary purpose is to facilitate the commercialization of technologies developed by one or more institutions of higher education.[188] These entities must file with the court a certification that they qualify for this exception and provide notice to the parties in the action.

Demand Letters

A patent demand letter is a letter sent by a patent-holder to a company or an individual accusing the recipient of patent infringement. The letters tend to demand that the alleged infringer take a specific action such as ceasing the infringing action or agreeing to a licensing arrangement. A patentee may use demand letters to prove willfulness in a patent infringement lawsuit, a high bar after recent court decisions. In the 2007 case, *In re Seagate Technology*, the Federal Circuit established a two-pronged test for willful infringement in a patent case. First, the patentee must show, by clear and convincing evidence, "that the infringer acted despite an objectively high likelihood that its actions constituted infringement of a valid patent."[189] Then the patentee must prove "subjective recklessness," which means that the accused infringer knew or should have known the risk of infringement.[190] A detailed demand letter, including a summary of the alleged patent infringement, helps to establish that the recipient/alleged infringer has the high degree of knowledge to meet this standard. Current law, however, does not dictate any specific content requirements or level of detail for demand letters.

The Innovation Act states that it is the "sense of Congress" that "it is an abuse of the patent system and against public policy for a party to send out purposely evasive demand letters to end users alleging patent infringement."[191] H.R. 9 also states that any claimant asserting willful infringement may not rely on demand letters as notification of infringement unless the letter identifies with particularity the asserted patent, the product or process accused, and the ultimate parent entity of the claimant, and explains how the product or process infringes to the extent possible.[192]

H.R. 1896, the "Demand Letter Transparency Act of 2015," outlines both content and disclosure requirements for demand letters. The bill would require any entity that sends 20 or more demand letters during any 365-day period to submit to the USPTO a disclosure identifying

- the patent, including a confirmation that the entity that sent the letter is the owner of the patent and is the last recorded entity in USPTO records for purposes of assignment, grant, or conveyance;
- the entity that has the right to license the patent or the name of the exclusive licensee;
- each entity asserting a claim with regard to the patent;
- each obligation to license the patent and the financial terms at which such patent has been licensed;
- the ultimate parent entity of such entity;
- the number of recipients of the letter;
- any case that has been filed by such entity relating to such patent; and
- any ex parte review or inter partes review of such patent.[193]

In order to enforce these proposed disclosure requirements, H.R. 1896 would permit a court in a patent infringement or validity action brought by an entity that does not meet such USPTO disclosure requirements to sanction such entity for an amount to be awarded to the adverse party to cover any costs incurred as a result of such violation.[194] The bill would exempt from these disclosure requirements original or joint inventors, institutions of higher education, and technology transfer organizations facilitating the commercialization of technology developed by institutions of higher education.[195]

In addition to the disclosure requirements, the Demand Letter Transparency Act of 2015 would require any demand letter sent to another entity to include specified information concerning

- each claim of each patent allegedly infringed, including each accused instrumentality;
- each party alleging infringement;
- the direct infringement for each claim alleged to have been infringed indirectly;
- the principal business of the party alleging infringement;

- each complaint filed that asserts or asserted any of the same patents, each case filed by such entity, and any ex parte or inter partes review for each patent;
- whether the patent is subject to any licensing term or pricing commitments;
- owners, co-owners, assignees, or exclusive licensees of the patent;
- any person who has a legal right to enforce the patent;
- any person with a direct financial interest in the outcome of the action; and
- how the recipient can access the USPTO demand letter database.[196]

Under the House's TROL Act[197] and the Senate's STRONG Patents Act,[198] a demand letter would qualify as an "unfair or deceptive act or practice" under the Federal Trade Commission Act[199] if the sender states or represents *wrongly* and *in bad faith* that

- the sender is a person with the right to license and enforce the patent;
- a civil action asserting a claim of infringement has been filed against the recipient;
- a civil action asserting a claim of infringement has been filed against other persons;
- legal action for infringement of the patent will be taken against the recipient;
- the sender is the exclusive licensee of the patent;
- persons other than the recipient purchased a license for the patent asserted in the letter;
- persons other than the recipient purchased an unrelated license and it is not identified as such;
- an investigation of the recipient's infringement occurred.[200]

The TROL Act and the STRONG Patents Act also would consider demand letters as unfair practices if the sender in bad faith seeks compensation for

- a patent that is held to be unenforceable or invalid in a final determination;
- activities taken by the recipient after expiration of the asserted patent;
- activity of the recipient that the sender knew was authorized by a person with the right to license the patent.[201]

Demand letters would also qualify as unfair practices under the TROL Act and the STRONG Patents Act if the sender fails to include

- the identity of the person including the name of the parent entity unless such person is a public company and the name of the public company is identified;
- an identification of at least one patent allegedly infringed;
- an identification of at least one product or service of the recipient infringing the identified patent;
- a name and contact information of a person the recipient may contact about the assertions or claims.[202]

Under both the TROL Act and the STRONG Patents Act, the Federal Trade Commission would enforce any violations of the provisions above.[203] This provision would also preempt any state law "expressly relating to the transmission or contents of communications relating to the assertion of patent rights."[204]

The Senate's PATENT Act addresses both abusive demand letters and demand letters sent as pre- suit notification. Section 9 of the Senate's PATENT Act would impose civil penalties on a person who has engaged in widespread abusive demand letter practices and has committed an unfair or deceptive act within the meaning of Section 5 of the Federal Trade Commission Act.[205] This bill outlines abusive demand letter practices as communications that falsely represent judicial relief or threaten litigation, and contain assertions that lack a reasonable basis in law or fact because the person does not have the right to assert the patent, the patent has expired, the patent is unenforceable, or the person has falsely represented that an infringement has occurred.[206] Similar to the enforcement provision outlined in the Senate's STRONG Patents Act, the Federal Trade Commission would enforce any violations of this particular provision. The Senate's PATENT Act would also require pre-suit notice letters that accuse a party of infringement to identify each patent believed to be infringed, to identify the allegedly infringing product, to describe why the plaintiff believes each patent identified is infringed, and to identify the person who can rightfully enforce the patent, as well as additional information.[207] The bill also states that if the plaintiff is seeking to establish willful infringement, then he may not rely on evidence of pre-suit notification of infringement unless that evidence includes this information.

On June 4, 2015, the Senate Judiciary Committee approved several amendments to the PATENT Act relating to demand letters, the most substantial of which would prohibit the pre-suit notice letter to contain (1) a request for, demand for, or offer to accept a specific monetary amount in exchange for a license, settlement, or similar agreement to resolve allegations of patent infringement; or (2) a specific monetary amount demanded based on the cost of legal defense in a lawsuit concerning any asserted claim.[208]

Commentators often associate vague demand letters with PAEs using these letters for the sole purpose of extracting financial concessions.[209] Supporters of more stringent requirements for demand letters point to vague demand letters as impediments of innovation due to the financial costs relating to litigation or settlement that ultimately arise from receiving these types of communications and the resulting impact on small businesses that cannot afford such costs.[210] Supporters also claim that placing more content-based requirements on demand letters would encourage patent owners to target specific infringers more carefully and likewise, would allow alleged infringers to have a clearer understanding of the infringement claims.[211] Critics of patent legislation have argued, however, that the legislation itself is not sufficiently tailored towards letters sent by PAEs, and additional requirements for patent letters may make "it more difficult for patent owners to communicate with potential licensees and alleged infringers even when those communications are in good faith."[212]

Reforms of Patent Trial and Appeal Board's Proceedings (IPR and PGR)

The Leahy-Smith America Invents Act (AIA)[213] established a new administrative proceeding conducted by the USPTO's Patent Trial and Appeal Board (PTAB) called a "post grant review" (PGR). In this proceeding, petitioners may challenge the validity of an issued patent based on any ground of patentability (such as unpatentable subject matter, or failure to meet the statutory standards of novelty and nonobviousness).[214] A petition to initiate a PGR must be filed within nine months of the date of patent grant.[215] To initiate a PGR, the petitioner must present information that, if not rebutted, would demonstrate that it is "more likely than not that at least one of the claims" is unpatentable.[216] A PGR must be completed within a year of its commencement, with an extension of six months possible for good cause shown.[217]

The AIA also created a new patent revocation proceeding called an "inter partes review" (IPR). A person who is not the patent owner may file a petition requesting inter partes review nine months after a patent issues or reissues, or the conclusion of any post-grant review, whichever occurs later.[218] In an IPR proceeding, petitioners may challenge the validity of an issued patent only on the basis of prior art consisting of patents or printed publications. As a result, patent challenges under IPR are limited to the patentability issues of novelty and nonobviousness.[219]

To initiate an IPR, the petitioner must demonstrate that there is a "reasonable likelihood" that he or she would prevail with respect to at least one claim.[220] An accused infringer may not petition for an IPR if he or she has already filed a declaratory judgment action in federal court challenging the patent, or more than a year has passed since the date the accused infringer was served with a complaint alleging infringement of that patent.[221] Should the patent survive the IPR proceeding, the individual who commenced the proceeding, along with his privies, are barred in the future from raising issues that were "raised or reasonably could have been raised."[222]

An IPR must be completed within a year of its commencement, with an extension of six months possible for good cause shown.[223]The timing and scope of the two USPTO patent revocation proceedings described above are as follows:

1. A patent may be challenged at the USPTO on any basis of any patentability issue within nine months from the date the patent issued (by filing a petition for a PGR proceeding).
2. Thereafter, and throughout its entire term, a patent may be challenged at the USPTO only on the grounds of novelty and nonobviousness (via an IPR).

Unlike most of the provisions in the patent litigation reform bills discussed above, which generally are to the benefit of defendants in patent infringement lawsuits, the reforms described in this section appear to favor patent holders who may have their patents challenged in an IPR or PGR; these changes have been championed by patent holders who, in particular, depend on patents to protect their business's revenue, such as brand-name pharmaceutical companies. However, because some of these changes would arguably make it more difficult to invalidate a patent in an IPR or PGR proceeding, patent assertion entities may also benefit from these amendments. Thus, the changes described below have been criticized as being "at odds" with the goal of addressing abusive patent litigation.[224] Nevertheless, such arguably conflicting reforms to the patent system appear to reflect the compromises that lawmakers believe are necessary to make in order to garner support for the legislation and help secure its passage.

Claim Construction Standard

The AIA is silent on what claim construction standard is appropriate in the IPR and PGR proceedings conducted by the PTAB. Pursuant to authority granted by the AIA, the USPTO promulgated a regulation in August 2012[225] that provided the following standard for claim construction in an IPR: "[a] claim in an unexpired patent shall be given its broadest reasonable construction in light of the specification of the patent in which it appears."[226] In a case issued in February 2015 involving a challenge to the USPTO's rulemaking authority to promulgate this regulation, a divided panel of the Federal Circuit upheld the PTAB's use of the "broadest reasonable interpretation" (BRI) standard in claim construction.[227] The appellate court noted that the USPTO has long applied the BRI standard in a variety of proceedings, including initial examinations, interferences, and reissue and reexamination proceedings.[228] The Federal Circuit explained that by applying the BRI standard, the USPTO "reduce[s] the possibility that, after the patent is granted, the claims may be interpreted as giving broader coverage than is justified."[229] The appellate court stated that "Congress is presumed to legislate against the background of existing law where Congress in enacting legislation is aware of the prevailing rule,"[230] and concluded that "Congress implicitly adopted the broadest reasonable interpretation standard in enacting the AIA."[231]

Section 9 of the Innovation Act and Section 11 of the PATENT Act (as reported) would legislatively overrule the Federal Circuit's recent decision regarding the use of the BRI standard in patent revocation proceedings. Instead, the Innovation Act and PATENT Act (as reported) would require that the PTAB, in IPR and PGR proceedings, use the same claim construction standard that is applied by federal courts; that is, the PTAB would need to construe a patent claim "in accordance with the ordinary and customary meaning of such claim as understood by one of ordinary skill in the art and the prosecution history pertaining to the patent."[232]

The Innovation Act and the PATENT Act (as reported) would also require the PTAB to consider prior claim construction by a court in a civil action in which the patent owner was a party.[233]

Sections 102 and 103 of the STRONG Patents Act contain similar amendments regarding the claim construction standard to be used in IPR and PGR proceedings. The PATENT Act does not include a provision that would alter the existing claim construction standard.

Former USPTO Director David Kappos has observed that currently, "the speed mandated for post-grant procedures is leading to greater interaction between court interpretations and USPTO interpretations of the same patent claims, and having the USPTO apply a different standard than the courts [for claim construction] is leading, and will continue to lead, to conflicting decisions."[234] However, he notes that there are valid arguments for retaining the broader standard for post-grant proceedings, such as that the BRI standard "requires patentees to define their claims clearly over the prior art during proceedings" before the USPTO.[235]

Others have asserted that changing the claim construction standard in IPR and PGR from BRI to "ordinary and customary meaning" would be a positive benefit to patent owners who feel that the BRI standard makes it easier to invalidate their patents in the AIA-established post-grant reviews than in federal courts.[236]

However, some groups oppose the inclusion of these changes to the IPR/PGR claim construction standard in the patent litigation reform bills, arguing that they "will undermine post grant review procedures that have proven to be an effective and useful tool in weeding out the weak patents that are often asserted in the most abusive of patent cases."[237] Technology companies have explained their opposition to the IPR/PGR amendments as follows:

> [T]he changes to the claim construction standard in IPR proceedings ... would eliminate a necessary and significant difference between the court system and USPTO standards for claim construction. In district court, the purpose is to determine liability for patent infringement; whereas the purpose of an IPR proceeding is for the USPTO to ensure its decision to issue a patent was, in fact, correct. The IPR process was amended in the AIA to provide a more streamlined, cost-effective method to challenge patent validity outside the court system. The proposed changes to this process endanger the meaningful progress Congress has made in reducing the burden invalid patents pose to our industry and will only make the process more costly and complex.[238]

Estoppel Effect of Unsuccessful Challenges in PGR Proceedings

An individual who commences a PGR proceeding, along with anyone who has a legal interest in the patent, are barred from raising in a later civil action issues that they raised in the administrative review of the validity of a patent claim—as well as any issue that "reasonably could have been raised" during the PGR.[239] Section 9 of the Innovation Act and Section 14(a) of the PATENT Act would narrow the estoppel effect arising from a PGR by removing the phrase "or reasonably could have raised" in the statute.[240] Thus, this provision would effectively permit parties to later assert in a civil action that a patent claim is invalid on any ground that the party "reasonably could have raised" during the PGR. The purpose of this change is apparently to correct an "inadvertent scrivener's error" made in drafting the AIA.[241]

Presumption of Validity and Burdens of Proof

The AIA provided that in an IPR or PGR proceeding, "the petitioner shall have the burden of proving a proposition of unpatentability by a preponderance of the evidence."[242] Sections 102(c) and 103(c) of the STRONG Patents Act would amend existing law to provide a presumption of validity to a previously issued claim that is challenged during an IPR or PGR proceeding.[243] These sections of the legislation would also heighten the evidentiary standard for proving unpatentability of a previously issued claim, requiring that the IPR or PGR petitioner prove such unpatentability "by clear and convincing evidence."[244]

The PATENT Act (as reported) would amend the statutory provisions governing evidentiary standards for IPR and PGR to provide that "the challenged patent shall be presumed to be valid."[245] However, the PATENT Act (as reported) does not change the evidentiary standard for proving unpatentability, as the STRONG Patents Act would. One observer has argued that "[a] presumption of validity combined with a preponderance of the evidence standard appears contradictory and creates an illogical process."[246]

Standing

On June 11, 2015, the House Judiciary Committee approved amendments to the Innovation Act that would prohibit the institution of an IPR or a PGR unless the petitioner certifies that the petitioner and the real parties in interest of the petitioner[247]

- do not own and will not acquire a financial instrument that is designed to hedge or offset any decrease in the market value of an equity security of the patent owner or an affiliate of the patent owner; and
- have not demanded payment (monetary or otherwise) from the patent owner or an affiliate of the patent owner in exchange for a commitment not to file a petition for IPR with respect to the owner's patent, unless the petitioner has been sued for or charged with infringement of the patent.

These changes are apparently in response to complaints made by pharmaceutical companies about so-called "reverse trolling" abuses of the PTAB proceedings, such as parties that threaten to challenge patents in IPR proceedings unless patent holders make substantial payments to them, or parties that have strategically used IPR to influence the stock prices of drug companies.[248]

Sections 102(d) and 103(d) of the STRONG Patents Act would provide even more stringent standing requirements for persons wanting to initiate a PGR or IPR. The legislation provides that in order to have standing to file a petition with the USPTO to institute an IPR,[249] a person, or a real party in interest or privy of the person, must show a reasonable possibility of being sued for, or charged with,[250] infringement of the patent. The STRONG Patents Act adjusts the standing requirement slightly for instituting a PGR:[251] a person, or a real party in interest or privy of the person, must demonstrate

- a reasonable possibility of being sued for, or charged with, infringement of the patent; or
- a competitive harm related to the validity of the patent.

Institution of an IPR/PGR Proceeding

The PATENT Act (as reported) would permit the USPTO Director to refuse to institute an IPR or PGR proceeding "if the Director determines that institution would not serve the interest of justice."[252] The Director would be required to consider several factors in making such determination, including

- whether the grounds of unpatentability are the same as those considered and decided in prior judicial or USPTO proceedings, and
- whether there is another proceeding or matter involving the same patent that is pending before the USPTO.

In addition, the PATENT Act (as reported) would require the USPTO Director to issue regulations governing the composition of panels convened to adjudicate a PGR or IPR, "to ensure that the panel adjudicating such proceeding consists of not more than 1 individual, if any, who participated in the decision to institute such proceeding."[253]

Ending Diversion of USPTO Fees

The USPTO is funded entirely by fees it charges to patent and trademark applicants, as well as other entities that interact with the agency.[254] However, the amounts received as fees by the USPTO must still be appropriated by Congress in order for the funds to be available to the agency for obligation or expenditure.[255] Yet over the past 25 years, Congress has often not allocated all of the fees that the USPTO has collected towards the operation of that agency. It has been estimated that, since 1999, over $1 billion in USPTO fee revenue has been withheld from the USPTO and directed towards unrelated government programs and operations.[256]

The America Invents Act (AIA) that was enacted in 2011 made several changes to the handling of fees collected by the USPTO. Under the AIA, the use of fees generated is still subject to the appropriations process, whereby Congress provides the budget authority for the USPTO to spend these fees. To address the issue of fees withheld from the office in the past, the AIA created within the Treasury a "Patent and Trademark Fee Reserve Fund" into which fee collections above that "appropriated by the Office for that fiscal year" are to be placed.[257] These funds are to be available to the USPTO "to the extent and in the amounts provided in appropriations Acts" and may only be used for the work of the USPTO.[258] However, the USPTO must still obtain congressional authority to use these "excess" funds.

Some argue that USPTO fee diversion is the "single most important problem facing our patent system today" because "continuing fee diversion constitute[s] a tax on innovation and undermine[s] efforts of the USPTO to reduce its backlog [of pending patent applications]."[259]

The STRONG Patents Act would put an end to USPTO fee diversion.[260] Section 107(a) of S. 632 would establish within the U.S. Treasury a revolving fund[261] called the "United States Patent and Trademark Office Innovation Promotion Fund" (Fund). Any fees collected by the USPTO would be deposited into this Fund and would be available to the USPTO Director until they are expended.[262] The amounts in the Fund would be available, without fiscal year limitation, to pay for all expenses of the USPTO, including all administrative and operating expenses that the office incurs.[263]

Venue

Title 28 of the U.S. Code, which governs the federal judicial system, contains a venue statute (Section 1400(b)) specifically applicable to patent cases, providing that "[a]ny civil action for patent infringement may be brought in the judicial district where the defendant resides, or where the defendant has committed acts of infringement and has a regular and established place of business."[264] However, a 1990 opinion by the Federal Circuit, *VE Holding Corp. v. Johnson Gas Appliance Co.,* applied the general federal venue statute (Section 1391(c)) to patent infringement cases, arguing that Congress, in amending the general venue statute in 1988, intended to change the scope of the patent venue statute in Section 1400(b):

> Other than by the clear language of the statute, Congress has not given any indication of whether it intended to change the scope of venue under § 1400(b). If we can infer anything from Congress' knowledge of the prior judicial interpretation of § 1400(b), given the clear language of the statute, it would be that Congress did intend to change the scope of venue under § 1400(b).[265]

VE Holding Corp. thus expanded venue in patent infringement cases beyond what is permitted by Section 1400(b), by allowing the filing of patent infringement lawsuits in "any district where there would be personal jurisdiction over the corporate defendant at the time the action is commenced."[266] In other words, defendants in patent cases could be sued wherever they offer products for sale. The Federal Circuit's liberalization of venue in patent cases has led to forum shopping, as plaintiffs (in particular patent assertion entities) seek to file infringement lawsuits in districts where judges and juries have reputations as being particularly favorable to patent holders, such as the Eastern District of Texas.[267]

The Innovation Act (as reported) would effectively overturn *VE Holding Corp.* by imposing limitations on the judicial districts in which a civil action may be brought for patent infringement or for a declaratory judgment that a patent is invalid or not infringed. The reason for this change is to "restore Congress's intent that patent infringement suits only be brought in judicial districts that have some reasonable connection to the dispute" and to "protect parties against the burden and inconvenience of litigating patent lawsuits in districts that are remote from any of the underlying events in the case."[268] The Innovation Act (as reported) would expressly exempt the special venue statute for patent actions from the applicability of the general venue statute (28 and would also revise it to allow an action relating to patents to be brought only in a judicial district[269]

1. where the defendant has its principal place of business or is incorporated
2. where the defendant has committed an act of infringement of a patent in suit and has a regular and established physical facility that gives rise to the act of infringement;
3. where the defendant has agreed or consented to be sued in the instant action;
4. where an inventor named on the patent in suit conducted research or development that led to the application for the patent in suit;
5. where a party has a regular and established physical facility that such party controls and operates (not primarily for the purpose of creating venue) and has
    a. engaged in management of significant research and development of an invention claimed in a patent in suit prior to the effective filing date of the patent;
    b. manufactured a tangible product that is alleged to embody an invention claimed in a patent in suit; or
    c. implemented a manufacturing process for a tangible good in which the process is alleged to embody an invention claimed in a patent in suit

The Innovation Act (as reported) would allow subsection (d) of the general venue statute (28 (d)) to govern venue for patent cases involving foreign defendants that are not incorporated in the United States or have no regular and established physical facilities in the United States.

Provisions Concerning Small Businesses

The patent reform litigation legislation introduced in the 114th Congress contains several provisions designed to help small businesses that are involved in the patent system either as patent owners or as defendants in infringement lawsuits.

Innovation Act and the PATENT Act

Section 7(a) of the Innovation Act and Section 12 of the PATENT Act would require the USPTO director to develop educational resources for small businesses with respect to their "concerns arising from patent infringement."[270] Furthermore, the Innovation Act would require that the USPTO's existing small business patent outreach programs, as well as relevant offices at the Small Business Administration and the Minority Business Development Agency, provide education and awareness on abusive patent litigation practices.[271] Section 7(b) of the Innovation Act and Section 12(b) of the PATENT Act would require the USPTO to create and maintain a "user-friendly" section of its official website, in which the public can find information about patent cases that have been filed in federal court and information about the patent at issue (including the disclosures regarding patent ownership that are mandated by the Innovation Act and PATENT Act). Neither bill authorizes or provides additional appropriations to pay for these initiatives; rather, they are to be implemented using existing agency resources.

Section 8(g) of the Innovation Act would require the USPTO director, in consultation with several heads of relevant agencies and interested parties, to conduct a study that examines the economic impact of the Innovation Act on the ability of individuals and small businesses owned by women, veterans, and minorities to enforce their patent rights. STRONG Patents Act

Section 111 of the STRONG Patents Act would require the Small Business Administration to produce a report that analyzes the impact of patent ownership by small businesses (those that are independently owned and operated and which are not dominant in their field of operation) and patent infringement actions against small businesses. In addition, the STRONG Patents Act would require the Director of the Administrative Office of the United States to designate at least six U.S. district courts (that are already participating in the patent cases pilot program) "for the purpose of that program to address special issues raised in patent infringement suits against individuals or small business concerns."[272] These specially designated courts would be required to expedite cases in which an individual or small business concern is accused of patent infringement.[273]

Table 1. Patent Litigation Reform Legislation in the 114th Congress

	H.R. 9 **Innovation Act (as reported)**	**S. 1137** **PATENT Act (as reported)**	**S. 632** **STRONG Patents Act**	**H.R. 1896** **Demand Letter Transparency Act**	**H.R. 2045** **TROL ACT**
Pleading Requirement	Proposed pleading requirements to include: • each patent allegedly infringed; • all claims necessary to identify each process, machine, manufacture, or composition of matter alleged to infringe any claim of each patent; • accused instrumentalities; • description of alleged infringement; • authority of plaintiff to assert patent General description of the above where information is not readily accessible Confidential information may be filed under seal ANDA suit exception	Proposed pleading requirements to include: • each patent allegedly infringed; • each claim of each patent allegedly infringed; • accused instrumentalities; • description of infringement General description where information is not available Confidential information may be filed under seal ANDA suit exception	n/a	n/a	n/a
Limits on Discovery	Postpone discovery if the defendant makes a motion to dismiss, transfer venue, or sever accused infringers Such motions must be filed within 90 days after service of the complaint and must include a declaration or other evidence in support of the motion	Discovery stayed pending court's ruling on defendant's motions to dismiss, transfer venue, or sever accused infringers; such motion must be filed prior to the first responsive pleading Court may allow limited discovery necessary to resolve those motions Court may allow additional	n/a	n/a	n/a

Table 1. (Continued)

	H.R. 9 Innovation Act (as reported)	S. 1137 PATENT Act (as reported)	S. 632 STRONG Patents Act	H.R. 1896 Demand Letter Transparency Act	H.R. 2045 TROL ACT
	Court may allow such discovery that the court deems is necessary to decide those motions Stay of discovery does not apply to an action in which patent holder seeks a preliminary injunction to prevent competitive harm Parties may also consent to exclusion from discovery limitations ANDA suit exception	discovery to preserve evidence or prevent prejudice to party Parties may consent to exclusion from discovery limitations ANDA suit exception			
Transparency of Patent Ownership	Upon filing of initial complaint for infringement, plaintiff must disclose to USPTO, court, and all adverse parties: • Assignee(s) of the patent • Entities with right to sublicense or enforce patent • Entities with financial interest in the patent (right to receive proceeds related to patent assertion) or in the plaintiff (direct or indirect ownership/control of more than 5% of the plaintiff) • Ultimate parent entities (UPE) of the above entities	Within 14 days of filing the complaint, plaintiff must notify court and adverse parties of: • Assignee(s) • Entities with right to sublicense or enforce patent • Entities with financial interest in the patent or in the plaintiff (direct or indirect ownership/control of > 20% of the plaintiff) • UPE of the above • List of other complaints filed in prior 3 years asserting the patent • Any licensing requirements that patent is subject to	n/a	n/a	n/a

	H.R. 9 Innovation Act (as reported)	S. 1137 PATENT Act (as reported)	S. 632 STRONG Patents Act	H.R. 1896 Demand Letter Transparency Act	H.R. 2045 TROL ACT
	• Description of the principal business of the plaintiff • List of all other complaints filed that assert the patent • Any licensing requirements that patent is subject to Plaintiff has an ongoing duty to notify USPTO of any changes in the above Failure to comply with duty of disclosure means plaintiff may not recover treble damages or reasonable fees during period of noncompliance; court may award fees to prevailing party for expenses incurred to uncover the updated information ANDA suit exception	Patentee may file this information under seal if confidential Patentee must file information regarding identity of entities with USPTO but no ongoing duty to update the information Assignment of all substantial rights in issued patent (and name of assignee and UPE) must be recorded in USPTO upon grant of patent and whenever subsequent assignments are made Same consequences as Innovation Act for failure to comply with duty to disclose assignment/UPE information to USPTO NO ANDA suit exception			
Stays of Customer-Suits	Court required to suspend/postpone litigation against customer if: • manufacturer is party to the civil action or in a separate action involving the patent • customer agrees to be bound by issues decided against the manufacturer • customer requests stay within the later of: 120 days after first	Court required to suspend/postpone litigation against customer if: • manufacturer is party to the civil action or in a separate action involving the patent • customer agrees to be bound by issues decided against the manufacturer • Consent of the manufacturer to the stay is needed only if manufacturer was made a party	n/a	n/a	n/a

Table 1. (Continued)

	H.R. 9 Innovation Act (as reported)	S. 1137 PATENT Act (as reported)	S. 632 STRONG Patents Act	H.R. 1896 Demand Letter Transparency Act	H.R. 2045 TROL ACT
	pleading is served, or the first scheduling order in the case Defines "customer" as a retailer or end user who has not materially modified the product/process alleged to infringe the patent Defines "end user" and "retailer" to exclude entities that manufacture the product/process at issue Stay may be lifted if suit against manufacturer will not resolve major issue in suit against customer or if stay unreasonably prejudices or is manifestly unjust to the party seeking to lift it ANDA suit exception	to the action on motion by the customer • customer requests stay within the later of: 90 days after first pleading is served, or the first scheduling order in the case Same definitions for "customer," "retailer," and "end user" as the Innovation Act (as reported) Same criteria as the Innovation Act for lift of the stay ANDA suit exception			
Shifting of Attorney Fees	Requires a court to award attorney fees to prevailing party unless court finds that either: • nonprevailing party's litigation position and conduct are "reasonably justified in law and fact" or • special circumstances exist that make an award unjust (special circumstances include undue	On motion of the prevailing party, court must determine whether the nonprevailing party's position was "objectively reasonable in law and fact" and whether its conduct was "objectively reasonable" • If they were not, court must award reasonable attorney fees to prevailing party unless special circumstances exist that make an award unjust	n/a	n/a	n/a

	H.R. 9 Innovation Act (as reported)	S. 1137 PATENT Act (as reported)	S. 632 STRONG Patents Act	H.R. 1896 Demand Letter Transparency Act	H.R. 2045 TROL ACT
	economic hardship to a named inventor) NO ANDA suit exception	• Special circumstances include undue economic hardship to a named inventor or to an institution of higher education The prevailing party shall bear the burden of demonstrating that the prevailing party is entitled to an award of attorney fees ANDA suit exception			
Attorney Fee Recovery	If nonprevailing party cannot pay, court shall join an interested party to pay if prevailing party shows that nonprevailing party has no substantial interest in the case other than asserting the patent Defendant must file initial statement expressing good faith belief that plaintiff has no substantial interest in the case other than asserting the patent Plaintiff must certify within 45 days of defendant's initial statement that: (a) the party has sufficient funds to pay for any potential fee award, (b) the party has substantial interest in the case other than asserting the patent, or (c) no other interested parties exist Court may deny motion to join interested party if: (a) interested party is not subject to service of	Defendant may file initial statement expressing good faith belief that the plaintiff's primary business is asserting patents Plaintiff must file a certification within 45 days of defendant's initial statement that includes: • that the party has sufficient funds to pay for any potential fee award, • that the party's primary business is not asserting/enforcing patents, • identity of interested parties, or • no such interested parties exist Plaintiff must provide interested parties notice that the party may be held accountable to pay for an award of attorney fees if the plaintiff cannot satisfy the full amount of the award			

Table 1. (Continued)

	H.R. 9 Innovation Act (as reported)	S. 1137 PATENT Act (as reported)	S. 632 STRONG Patents Act	H.R. 1896 Demand Letter Transparency Act	H.R. 2045 TROL ACT
	process, or (b) joinder would deprive court of subject matter jurisdiction or make venue improper Court must deny motion to join interested party if: (a) party did not receive timely notice of being identified as an interested party, or (b) interested party renounces in writing and with notice to the court and parties, any ownership, right, or direct financial interest in the patent Exceptions for: university tech transfer organizations	Interested parties may avoid financial liability by renouncing their interest in the patent, within 120 days of receipt of the notice above Interested parties may intervene in the action to contest its identification as an interested party or their liability for attorney fees Court may exempt interested party from liability in the interest of justice Exceptions for: universities, non-profit tech transfer organizations, and ANDA suits	n/a	n/a	n/a
Demand Letters	"Sense of Congress" that action including litigation stemming from purposely evasive demand letter should be considered fraudulent or deceptive practice	Party may not rely on evidence of pre-suit notification to establish willful infringement unless communication contains specific information Prohibits pre-suit notification from containing statements that: request, demand, or offer to accept a specific monetary amount in exchange for a license, settlement, or similar agreement to resolve	Defines a demand letter as an unfair or deceptive practice under FTC Act if wrongly and in bad faith misrepresents specific details	Entity that sends 20 or more demand letters per year must disclose specific information to USPTO Demand letters must include specific information relating to the patent claim	Defines a demand letter as a unfair or deceptive practice under FTC Act if wrongly and in bad faith misrepresents

	H.R. 9 Innovation Act (as reported)	S. 1137 PATENT Act (as reported)	S. 632 STRONG Patents Act	H.R. 1896 Demand Letter Transparency Act	H.R. 2045 TROL ACT
		allegations of patent infringement; or • demand a specific monetary amount based on the cost of legal defense in a lawsuit concerning any asserted claim Defines widespread demand letter abuse as violation of FTC Act		allegedly infringed and the party alleging infringement	specific details
Reforms of PTAB's IPR and PGR Proceedings	Requires the Patent Trial and Appeal Board (PTAB), in inter parties review (IPR) and post-grant review (PGR) proceedings, to follow the same claim construction standard used by district courts Narrows the estoppel effect arising from a PGR by allowing a PGR petitioner to raise in a later civil action issues (with respect to the validity of a patent claim) that they "reasonably could have raised" during the PGR Prohibits IPR or PGR from being initiated unless petitioner certifies that the petitioner: • does not own and will not acquire a financial instrument that is designed to hedge or offset any decrease in the market value of an equity security of the patent owner or an affiliate of the patent owner; and	Requires the PTAB, in IPR and PGR proceedings, to follow the same claim construction standard used by district courts Narrows the estoppel effect arising from a PGR by allowing a PGR petitioner to raise in a later civil action issues (with respect to the validity of a patent claim) that they "reasonably could have raised" during the PGR Clarifies that the patent challenged in an IPR or PGR shall be presumed to be valid Allows the USPTO Director to refuse to institute an IPR or PGR proceeding "if the Director determines that institution would not serve the interest of justice;" factors relevant to such determination include: • whether the grounds of unpatentability are the same as	Requires the PTAB, in IPR and PGR proceedings, to follow the same claim construction standard used by district courts Provides a presumption of validity to a previously issued claim that is challenged during an IPR or PGR proceeding Requires IPR/PGR petitioner to prove unpatentability of a previously issued claim "by clear and convincing evidence" (existing law is		

Table 1. (Continued)

	H.R. 9 Innovation Act (as reported)	S. 1137 PATENT Act (as reported)	S. 632 STRONG Patents Act	H.R. 1896 Demand Letter Transparency Act	H.R. 2045 TROL ACT
	• has not demanded payment (monetary or otherwise) from the patent owner or an affiliate of the patent owner in exchange for a commitment not to file a petition for IPR with respect to the owner's patent, unless the petitioner has been sued for or charged with infringement of the patent	those considered and decided in prior judicial or USPTO proceedings, and • whether there is another proceeding or matter involving the same patent that is pending before the USPTO Requires that panels convened to adjudicate PGR or IPR proceedings have no more than 1 person, if any, who participated in the decision to institute such proceeding	"preponderance of the evidence") Provides more stringent standing requirements for IPR/PGR petitioner	n/a	n/a
Elimination of USPTO Fee Diversion	n/a	n/a	Establishes a revolving fund in which fees collected by USPTO would be deposited; such fees would be available to USPTO until expended	n/a	n/a
Venue	Limited to judicial districts where: • defendant has its principal place of business or is incorporated; • defendant has committed anact of infringement of a patent in	n/a	n/a	n/a	n/a

	H.R. 9 Innovation Act (as reported)	S. 1137 PATENT Act (as reported)	S. 632 STRONG Patents Act	H.R. 1896 Demand Letter Transparency Act	H.R. 2045 TROL ACT
	suit and has a regular and established physical facility that gives rise to the act of infringement; • defendant has agreed or consented to be sued in the instant action; • where inventor named on the patent in suit conducted research or development that led to the application for the patent in suit; • a party has a regular and established physical facility that such party controls/operates and has engaged in significant research and development of, or manufactured a tangible product that is alleged to embody, the invention claimed in the patent General venue statute (28 U.S.C. §1391(d)) governs venue for patent cases involving foreign defendants that are not incorporated or have no regular and established physical facilities in the United States				
Small Business	Requires USPTO director to develop educational resources for small businesses with respect to their "concerns arising from patent infringement"	Requires USPTO director to develop educational resources for small businesses with respect to their "concerns arising from patent infringement"	Requires Small Business Administration to produce a report analyzing the	n/a	n/a

Table 1. (Continued)

	H.R. 9 Innovation Act (as reported)	S. 1137 PATENT Act (as reported)	S. 632 STRONG Patents Act	H.R. 1896 Demand Letter Transparency Act	H.R. 2045 TROL ACT
	Requires USPTO and other federal agencies to provide, through existing small business outreach programs, education and awareness on abusive litigation practices Requires USPTO to create and maintain a "user-friendly" section of its website in which the public may find information about filed patent cases and the patents at issue in those cases Requires USPTO director to conduct a study examining the economic impact of the Innovation Act on the ability of individuals and small businesses owned by women, veterans, and minorities to enforce their patent rights	Requires USPTO to create and maintain a "user-friendly" section of its website in which the public may find information about filed patent cases and the patents at issue in those cases	impact of patent ownership by small businesses and patent infringement actions against small businesses Requires Director of the Administrative Office to designate at least six district courts to address special issues raised in patent infringement suits against individuals or small business concerns; such courts would be required to expedite cases in which an individual or small business concern is accused of patent infringement		

Source: Congressional Research Service.

End Notes

[1] Portions of this report have been borrowed and adapted from CRS Report R42668, *An Overview of the "Patent Trolls" Debate*, by Brian T. Yeh and CRS Report R43321, *Patent Infringement Pleadings: An Analysis of Recent Proposals for Patent Reform*, by Emily M. Lanza.

[2] H.R. 9, the Innovation Act: Hearing Before the House Judiciary Comm., 114th Cong., 1st Sess. (2015); S. 1137, the "PATENT ACT"—Finding Effective Solutions to Address Abusive Patent Practices: Hearing Before the Senate Judiciary Comm., 114th Cong. 1st Sess. (2015); H.R., the Targeting Rogue and Opaque Letters Act (TROL Act): Hearing Before the House Energy and Commerce Comm., Subcomm. on Commerce, Manufacturing, and Trade, 114th Cong. 1st Sess. (2015); Patent Reform: Protecting American Innovators and Job Creators from Abusive Patent Litigation: Hearing Before the House Judiciary Comm., Subcomm. on Courts, Intellectual Property and Internet, 114th Cong. 1st Sess. (2015); The Impact of Abusive Patent Litigation Practices on the American Economy: Hearing Before the Senate Judiciary Comm., 114th Cong. 1st Sess. (2015); Patent Reform: Protecting Innovation and Entrepreneurship: Hearing Before the Senate Comm. on Small Business and Entrepreneurship, 114th Cong. 1st Sess. (2015); Trolling for a Solution: Ending Abusive Patent Demand Letters: Hearing Before the House Energy and Commerce Comm., Subcomm. on Commerce, Manufacturing, and Trade, 113th Cong. 2d Sess. (2014); H.R. 3309, the "Innovation Act:" Hearing Before the House Judiciary Comm., 113th Cong., 1st Sess. (2013); Protecting Small Businesses and Promoting Innovation by Limiting Patent Troll Abuse: Hearing Before the Senate Judiciary Comm., 113th Cong., 1st Sess.(2013); The Impact of Patent Assertion Entities on Innovation and the Economy: Hearing Before the House Energy and Commerce Comm., Subcomm. on Oversight and Investigations, 113th Cong., 1st Sess. (2013); Demand Letters and Consumer Protection: Examining Deceptive Practices by Patent Assertion Entities: Hearing Before the Senate Commerce, Science, and Transportation Comm., Subcomm. on Consumer Protection, Product Safety, and Insurance, 113th Cong., 1st Sess. (2013); Abusive Patent Litigation: The Issues Impacting American Competitiveness and Job Creation at the International Trade Commission and Beyond: Hearing Before the House Judiciary Comm., Subcomm. on Courts, Intellectual Property, and the Internet, 113th Cong., 1st Sess. (2013); Abusive Patent Litigation: The Impact on American Innovation and Jobs, and Potential Solutions: Hearing Before the House Judiciary Comm., Subcomm. on Courts, Intellectual Property, and the Internet, 113th Cong., 1st Sess. (2013).

[3] In the 114th Congress, introduced legislation includes the Innovation Act (H.R. 9), Protecting American Talent and Entrepreneurship Act (PATENT) Act (S. 1137), Demand Letter Transparency Act of 2015 (H.R. 1896), Targeting Rogue and Opaque Letters (TROL) Act (H.R. 2045), and the Support Technology and Research for Our Nation's Growth (STRONG) Patents Act of 2015 (S. 632). In the 113th Congress, legislation that was introduced but not enacted included the following: the Innovation Act (H.R. 3309), Transparency in Assertion of Patents Act (S. 2049), the Patent Transparency and Improvements Act of 2013 (S. 1720), the Patent Abuse Reduction Act of 2013 (S. 1013), the Patent Litigation Integrity Act of 2013 (S. 1612), the Demand Letter Transparency Act of 2013 (H.R. 3540), Patent Litigation and Innovation Act of 2013 (H.R. 2639), End of Anonymous Patents Act (H.R. 2024), and the Saving High-Tech Innovators from Egregious Legal Disputes (SHIELD) Act of 2013 (H.R. 845).

[4] The House Judiciary Committee reported H.R. 9 on July 29, 2015, *see* H.Rept. 114-235. The Senate Judiciary Committee reported S. 1137 on September 8, 2015.

[5] 35 U.S.C. §101.

[6] Diamond v. Diehr, 450 U.S. 175, 185 (1981).

[7] 35 U.S.C. §131.

[8] *Id.* §112.
[9] 3-8 DONALD S. CHISUM, CHISUM ON PATENTS §8.01 (2006).
[10] 35 U.S.C. §§102, 103(a).
[11] *Id.* §102.
[12] "Prior art" is a legal term of art that refers to the materials (usually called "references" in patent law) that comprise the available knowledge regarding the subject matter of the invention sought to be patented, such as other issued patents, publications, and evidence of actual uses or sales of the technology. ROGER SCHECHTER AND JOHN THOMAS, PRINCIPLES OF PATENT LAW 4-1 (2d ed. 2004).
[13] 35 U.S.C. §103(a).
[14] In re Fischer, 421 F.3d 1365, 1371 (Fed. Cir. 2005).
[15] 35 U.S.C. §§154(a)(1), 271(a).
[16] *Id.* §271(a).
[17] *Id.* §283.
[18] *Id.* §284.
[19] *Id.* §154(a)(2).
[20] *Id.* §261.
[21] ROGER SCHECHTER AND JOHN THOMAS, PRINCIPLES OF PATENT LAW §11-1 (2d ed. 2004).
[22] A patent holder has the right to exclude others from making, using, offering for sale, or selling the invention throughout the United States, or importing the protected invention into the United States. 35 U.S.C. §154(a)(1).
[23] SCHECHTER AND THOMAS, *supra* footnote 21, §11-1.
[24] United States v. General Electric Co., 272 U.S. 476, 490 (1926).
[25] JOHN R. THOMAS, PHARMACEUTICAL PATENT LAW 427 (BNA Books 2005).
[26] 28 U.S.C. §1295(a)(1).
[27] *Id.* §1254(1).
[28] Colleen V. Chien, *Patently Protectionist,* 50 WILLIAM AND MARY L. REV. 63, 70 (2008) (patent cases comprise 85% of the ITC's Section 337 docket). For more information about Section 337 proceedings, *see* CRS Report RS22880, *Intellectual Property Rights Protection and Enforcement: Section 337 of the Tariff Act of 1930*, by Shayerah Ilias Akhtar.
[29] 35 U.S.C. §282.
[30] For more on declaratory judgment actions in patent cases, see CRS Report RL34156, *A Nonrepudiating Patent Licensee's Right To Seek Declaratory Judgment of Invalidity or Noninfringement of the Licensed Patent: MedImmune v. Genentech*, by Brian T. Yeh.
[31] The requirement that an immediate, concrete dispute between the patent owner and another individual arises because the U.S. Constitution vests the federal courts with jurisdiction only where a "case or controversy" exists. U.S. CONST., Art. III, Sec. 2, cl. 1. A charge of patent infringement typically satisfies the "case or controversy" requirement. See Prasco, LLC v. Medicis Pharm. Corp., 537 F.3d 1329 (Fed. Cir. 2008).
[32] The PTAB's membership consists of the USPTO director, deputy director, the Commissioner for Patents, the Commissioner for Trademarks, and the administrative patent judges. 35 U.S.C. §6(a).
[33] The USPTO provides a helpful chart that compares the major differences between the three administrative trials, in terms of (1) who may file a petition with the USPTO to institute the review; (2) when such a petition is allowed; (3) the estoppel provisions applicable to the review (to prevent individuals from making repetitive arguments during later proceedings—either in federal court, the ITC, or in a USPTO administrative proceeding); (4) standards to trigger the review; (5) the standard to prove invalidity; (6) time limits for completing the review; and (7) the basis for challenging validity of the patent, *available at* http://beta.uspto.gov/sites/default/files/ip/boards/bpai/ aia_trial_comparison_chart.pptx.
[34] 35 U.S.C. §§318(b); 328(b).
[35] For comprehensive background information on these entities, *see* CRS Report R42668, *An Overview of the "Patent Trolls" Debate*, by Brian T. Yeh.

[36] FEDERAL TRADE COMMISSION, THE EVOLVING IP MARKETPLACE: ALIGNING PATENT NOTICE AND REMEDIES WITH COMPETITION 67-68 (2011).

[37] *See* Gerard N. Magliocca, *Blackberries and Barnyards: Patent Trolls and the Perils of Innovation*, 82 NOTRE DAME L. REV. 1809 (2007).

[38] John R. Allison, Mark A. Lemley and Joshua Walker, *Patent Quality and Settlement Among Repeat Patent Litigants*, 99 GEO. L.J. 677, 694 (2011).

[39] The term was coined at Intel in 2001 as a pithy label for litigants asserting patents that they owned but did not practice and which they typically acquired. An Intel Corporation vice president had been sued after referring to such litigants as "patent extortionists." *See* Joff Wild, *The Real Inventors of the Term "Patent Troll" Revealed*, IAM MAGAZINE, August 22, 2008, http://iam-magazine.com/blog/detail.aspx?g=cff2afd3-c24e-42e5-aa68-a4b4e7524177.

[40] *See, e.g.*, Ronald S. Katz et al., *Patent Trolls: A Selective Etymology*, IP LAW 360, March 20, 2008, http://manatt.com/uploadedFiles/News_and_Events/Articles_By_Us/patentroll.pdf; *see also* Jenna Greene, *Trolls? Patent Director Says the Term Isn't Helpful,* NAT'L LAW JOURNAL, January 22, 2015 (quoting USPTO Director Michelle Lee: "I don't find the term [patent troll] helpful. It means different things to different people. We need to focus on behavior.").

[41] Nathan Myhrvold, *The Big Idea: Funding Eureka!*, HARV. BUS. REV. 44 (2010).

[42] *Id.* at 48–49; Sannu K. Shrestha, *Trolls or Market-Maker? An Empirical Analysis of Nonpracticing Entities*, 110 COLUM. L. REV. 114, 126–30 (2010); FTC Report, *supra* note 36, at 64, 68.

[43] *See, e.g.,* James Bessen et. al., *The Private and Social Costs of Patent Trolls*, REGULATION 26, 34 (2006); Elizabeth D. Ferrill, *Patent Investment Trusts: Let's Build a PIT to Catch the Patent Trolls*, 6 N.C. J.L. and TECH. 367, 371–374 (2005).

[44] Bessen et. al, *supra* note 43, at 34.

[45] FTC Report, *supra* note 36, at 40 n. 43.

[46] Ferrill, *supra* note 43, *at* 371–374.

[47] *See, e.g.,* Bessen et. al, *supra* note 43, at 31-35.

[48] EXECUTIVE OFFICE OF THE PRESIDENT, PATENT ASSERTION AND U.S. INNOVATION 1 (June 2013), *at* https://www.whitehouse.gov/sites/default/files/docs/patent_report.pdf.

[49] *See, e.g.,* Ron Epstein, *Debunking the 'Patent Troll' Myth*, BLOOMBERG BUSINESSWEEK, August 15, 2011, *available at* http:// www.businessweek.com/ stories/ 2010-02-01/ debunking-the-patent-troll-mythbusinessweek-business-news-stock-market-and-financial-advice.

[50] In the *primary* market for *technology*, revenue and returns on investment come from commercializing the patented technology and exploiting exclusive rights to use it in the marketplace. In the *secondary* market for *patents*, revenue comes from licensing fees. PAEs sell or license their patents "as assets whose values are based on the amount of licensing fees that can be extracted from operating companies already using and marketing the technology." *See* FTC Report, *supra* note 36, at 60.

[51] Smaller inventors may lack the resources or know-how to commercialize, and it will often be inefficient for them to try. Other patents may not become valuable for years or require further capital and sunk costs.

[52] U.S. Supreme Court Order, April 2015.

[53] As previously discussed, patent infringement is the unauthorized making, using, offering for sale, selling, and importing of a patented invention. 35 U.S.C. §271.

[54] Fed. R. Civ. P. Form 18.

[55] K-Tech Telecommunications v. Time Warner Cable, 714 F.3d 1278 (Fed. Cir. 2013).

[56] McZeal v. Sprint Nextel Corp., 501 F.3d 1354, 1358 (Fed. Cir. 2007).

[57] *Id.*

[58] Ashcroft v. Iqbal, 556 U.S. 662 (2009).

[59] Bell Atl. Corp. v. Twombly, 550 U.S. 544 (2007).

[60] Iqbal, 556 U.S. at 678; Twombly, 550 U.S. at 556.

[61] In re Bill of Lading Transmission and Process System Patent Litigation, 681 F.3d 1323, 1334 (Fed. Cir. 2012).

[62] *Id.*

[63] As originally introduced, H.R. 9 would have required "[a]n identification of each claim of each patent ... that is allegedly infringed" (which is also the same information required by the PATENT Act). However, the Manager's Amendment to the Innovation Act that was approved by the House Judiciary Committee on June 11, 2015, replaces that language with the text described above, thereby lowering the standard of this particular pleading requirement.

[64] H.R. 9, §3, *adding new* 35 U.S.C. §281A.

[65] S. 1137, §3, *adding new* 35 U.S.C. §281A.

[66] *Id., adding new* 35 U.S.C. §281B.

[67] *Id.*

[68] H.R. 9, §6; S. 1137, §3. The Supreme Court's order abolishing Form 18 went into effect on December 1, 2015 absent congressional action.

[69] H.R. 9, §3, *adding new* 35 U.S.C. §281A; S. 1137, §3, *adding new* 35 U.S.C. §281A.

[70] The Innovation Act and the PATENT Act provide an exception to this disclosure requirement for civil actions that include a specific cause of action for patent infringement involving pharmaceutical drugs. The particular cause of action, established by the Hatch-Waxman Act and codified in 35 U.S.C. §271(e)(2), allows a brand-name drug company to enforce its patents against a potential generic competitor at such time that the generic firm files an application (a so-called Abbreviated New Drug Application (ANDA)) with the Food and Drug Administration, seeking marketing approval. For more information on this provision, *see* CRS Report R42354, *Patent Infringement and Experimental Use Under the Hatch-Waxman Act: Current Issues*, by John R. Thomas.

[71] *See, e.g.,* Patent Progress, *Common Sense Solutions to the Patent Control Problem, at* http://www.patentprogress.org/ patent-troll-reform/common-sense-solutions-to-the-patent-troll-problem/.

[72] H.Rept. 113-279, at 23.

[73] *Id.*

[74] *Id.*

[75] *See* Edward R. Ergenzinger and Andrew R. Shores, "Here We Go Again: The Next Round of Legislative Patent Law Reform," *at* http://www.wardandsmith.com/articles/the-next-round-of-legislative-patent-law-reform.

[76] Discovery is the process to gather information in preparation for trial.

[77] *See* Fed. R. Civ. P. 26.

[78] *See* Chief Judge Randall R. Rader, *The State of Patent Litigation,* Eastern District of Texas Bar Association Judicial Conference, September 27, 2011.

[79] This type of hearing developed as the result of the U.S. Supreme Court decision in *Markman v. Westview Instruments, Inc.*, 517 U.S. 370 (1996).

[80] *See* Phillips v. AWH Corp., 415 F.3d 1303 (Fed. Cir. 2005).

[81] H.R. 9 (as reported), §3(d), *adding new* 35 U.S.C. §281B(a). As introduced, the Innovation Act would have required that hearings relating to patent claim construction occur prior to significant fact discovery, as the bill would have limited discovery "to information necessary for the court to determine the meaning of the terms used in the patent claim." H.R. 9 (as introduced), §3, *adding new* 35 U.S.C. §299A. In addition, the Innovation Act (as introduced) would have granted courts with the discretion to permit discovery "in special circumstances" to prevent manifest injustice. *Id.*

[82] H.R. 9 (as reported), §3(d), *adding new* 35 U.S.C. §281B(d).

[83] S. 1137, §4, *adding new* 35 U.S.C. §299B.

[84] *Id.*

[85] H.Rept. 113-279, at 9.

[86] *The Impact of Abusive Patent Litigation Practices on the American Economy: Hearing Before the Senate Judiciary Comm.*, 114th Cong., 1st Sess. (2015) (Statement of Hans Sauer, Deputy General Counsel for Intellectual Property, Biotechnology Industry Organization).

[87] *Innovation Alliance Priority Positions on S. 1137, the Senate Protecting American Talent and Entrepreneurship (PATENT) Act,* May 6, 2015, *at* http://innovationalliance.net/from-the-alliance/innovation-alliance-priority-positions-s- 1137-senate-protecting-american-talent-entrepreneurship-patent-act/.

[88] This topic is often referred to as the disclosure of the "real party-in-interest."

[89] 35 U.S.C. §290.

[90] H.R. 9, §4(a)(3), *adding new* 35 U.S.C. §290(b)(2).

[91] The Innovation Act defines "financial interest" to mean (1) with regard to a patent, the right of a person to receive proceeds related to the assertion of the patent(s), and (2) with regard to the plaintiff, direct or indirect ownership or control by a person of more than 5% of such plaintiff. H.R. 9, §4(a)(3), *adding new* 35 U.S.C. §290(e)(1). However, the definition expressly excludes anyone who owns shares or other interests in a mutual or common investment fund (unless the person participates in the management of such fund) and also excludes the proprietary interest of a policyholder in a mutual insurance company or of a depositor in a mutual savings association, unless the outcome of the civil action could substantially affect the value of that proprietary interest.

[92] The Innovation Act defines "ultimate parent entity" by reference to 16 C.F.R. §801.1(a)(3), which provides that the term "means an entity which is not controlled by any other entity." H.R. 9, §4(a)(3), *adding new* 35 U.S.C. §290(e)(3).

[93] Additional required information added by the Manager's Amendment to the Innovation Act, which was approved by the House Judiciary Committee. *See* H.R. 9 (as reported), §4(a)(3), *adding new* 35 U.S.C. §290(b)(1)(E).

[94] *Id., adding new* 35 U.S.C. §290(b)(1)(F).

[95] *Id., adding new* 35 U.S.C. §290(b)(1)(G).

[96] H.R. 9, §4(a)(3), *adding new* 35 U.S.C. §290(d)(1).

[97] *Id., adding new* 35 U.S.C. §290(d)(2)(A).

[98] *Id., adding new* 35 U.S.C. §290(d)(2)(B).

[99] *Id.* §4(c).

[100] *Press Release: Goodlatte, Defazio, Issa, Nadler, Smith, Lofgren, Eshoo Introduce Patent Litigation Reform Bill,* February 5, 2015, *available at* http:// judiciary.house.gov/ index.cfm/2015/2/goodlatte-defazio-issa-nadler-smith-lofgren-eshoo-introduce-patent-litigation-reform-bill.

[101] Howard Klein, *Patent Law Reform—Proceed with Caution,* Law360.com, March 9, 2015, *at* http://www.law360.com/articles/626618/patent-law-reform-proceed-with-caution.

[102] *Id.*

[103] S. 1137, §3(b)(1), *adding new* 35 U.S.C. §281B(b). However, unlike the Innovation Act, the PATENT Act would NOT create an exception to the patent ownership disclosure requirement for a civil action that includes a cause of action for patent infringement under 35 U.S.C. §271(e)(2).).

[104] The PATENT Act uses the same definition for "ultimate parent entity" as the Innovation Act.

[105] The PATENT Act defines the term "financial interest" in a similar fashion to the Innovation Act, except that S. 1137 would, with regard to the patentee, apply the term to persons who have "direct or indirect ownership or control" of more than 20% of the patentee (compared to the Innovation Act's 5%).

[106] For more information about the promise of members of standard-setting organizations to license certain patented inventions to others on "fair, reasonable, and nondiscriminatory (FRAND) terms," *see* CRS Report R42705, *Availability of Injunctive Relief for Standard-Essential Patent Holders*, by Brian T. Yeh.

[107] *Id., adding new* 35 U.S.C. §281B(e).

[108] *Id.* §3(b)(1), *adding new* 35 U.S.C. §281B(d).

[109] *Id.* §10(a), *adding new* 35 U.S.C. §261(A)(b), (c).

[110] *Id., adding new* 35 U.S.C. §261(A)(d).

[111] *Id.*

[112] *Id.* §10(b).

[113] 35 U.S.C. §271(a) (emphasis added).

[114] *See* Aro Mfg. Co., Inc. v. Convertible Top Replacement Co., Inc., 377 U.S. 476, 484 (1964) (explaining that "it has often and clearly been held that unauthorized use, without more, constitutes infringement.").

[115] *See* Colleen V. Chien and Edward Reines, *Why Technology Customers Are Being Sued en Masse for Patent Infringement and What Can Be Done* (Santa Clara Univ. Sch. of L. Legal Studies Research Papers Series, Working Paper No. 20-13, 2013), *available at* http://papers.ssrn.com/sol3/papers.cfm?abstract_id=2318666.

[116] *Abusive Patent Litigation: The Impact on American Innovation and Jobs, and Potential Solutions: Hearing Before the House Judiciary Comm., Subcomm. on Courts, Intellectual Property, and the Internet,* 113th Cong., 1st Sess. (2013) (Statement of Philip S. Johnson, Chief Intellectual Property Counsel, Johnson and Johnson, on behalf of the 21st Century Coalition for Patent Reform), at 7, *available at* http:// judiciary.house.gov/ _files/ hearings/ 113th/03142013_2/ Johnson%2003142013.pdf.

[117] Spread Spectrum Screening LLC v. Eastman Kodak Co., 657 F.3d 1349, 1357 (Fed. Cir. 2011).

[118] Codex Corp. v. Milgo Electronic Corp., 553 F.2d 735 (1st Cir.), *cert. denied*, 434 U.S. 860 (1977).

[119] Brian J. Love and James C. Yoon, *Expanding Patent Law's Customer Suit Exception,* 93 B.U. L. REV. 1605, 1614 (October 2013), citing Katz v. Lear Siegler, Inc., 909 F.2d 1459 (Fed. Cir. 1990).

[120] H.R. 9, §5(a), replacing existing 35 U.S.C. §296 that contains an unrelated provision that attempted to make state governments and state institutions liable for monetary damages in a patent infringement lawsuit. This provision that sought to abrogate a state's Eleventh Amendment sovereign immunity has been invalidated by the Supreme Court in a 1999 decision, *Florida Prepaid v. College Savings Bank*, 527 U.S. 627 (1999). For more information on this issue, *see* CRS Report RL34593, *Infringement of Intellectual Property Rights and State Sovereign Immunity*, by Brian T. Yeh.

[121] H.R. 9 (as reported), §5(a), *adding revised* 35 U.S.C. §296(b)(1)-(3). As originally introduced, the Innovation Act would have required both the manufacturer of the product and the customer to consent to the stay of the action in writing. H.R. 9 (as introduced), *adding revised* 35 U.S.C. §296(a)(1).

[122] *Id., adding revised* 35 U.S.C. §296(c).

[123] *Id., adding revised* 35 U.S.C. §296(d).

[124] H.Rept. 113-279, p. 30.

[125] S. 1137, §4, *adding new* 35 U.S.C. §299A.

[126] H.R. 9 (as reported), §5, *adding revised* 35 U.S.C. §296(b)(4); S. 1137, §4, *adding new* 35 U.S.C. §299A(c).

[127] S. 1137, §4, *adding new* 35 U.S.C. §299A(d).

[128] *Id., adding new* 35 U.S.C. §299A(b).

[129] Marx v. General Revenue Corp., 133 S. Ct. 1166, 1175 (2013); *see also* Alyeska Pipeline Service Co. v. Wilderness Society, 421 U.S. 240, 247-53 (1975) (explaining that "[i]n the United States, the prevailing litigant is ordinarily not entitled to collect a reasonable attorneys' fee from the loser.").

[130] Brooks Furniture Mfg., Inc. v. Dutailier Intern., Inc., 393 F.3d 1378 (Fed. Cir. 2005) (*overruled by* Octane Fitness, LLC v. ICON Health and Fitness, Inc., No. 12-1184, slip op. (2014)).

[131] *Id.* at 1382.

[132] *See* Randall R. Rader et al., *Make Patent Trolls Pay in Court,* N.Y. TIMES, June 4, 2013, *available at* http://www.nytimes.com/2013/06/05/opinion/make-patent-trolls-pay-in-court.html?_r=0 (noting that "fees were shifted under Section 285 in only 20 out of nearly 3,000 patent cases filed in 2011.").

[133] Octane Fitness, LLC v. ICON Health and Fitness, Inc., No. 12-1184, slip op. at 1 (2014).

[134] *Id.* at 7.

[135] *Id.* at 8.

[136] *Id.* at 11.

[137] Highmark Inc. v. Allcare Health Mgmt.Sys., No. 12-1163, slip. op. (2014).

[138] *Id.* at 5.

[139] Daniel Fisher, *Patent Trolls Face Higher Risks As Supreme Court Loosens Fee-Shifting Rule,* Forbes, April 29, 2014, *at* http://www.forbes.com/sites/danielfisher/2014/04/29/patent-trolls-face-higher-risks-as-supreme-court-loosens- fee-shifting-rule/.

[140] *Examining Recent Supreme Court Cases in the Patent Area: Hearing Before the House Judiciary Comm., Subcomm. on Courts, Intellectual Property, and the Internet,* 114th Cong., 1st Sess. (2015) (Statement of Andrew J. Pincus, Partner, Mayer Brown LLP), at 3, *available at* http://judiciary.house.gov/_cache/files/43c13fd8-8287-4a3f-b172- 67a0b37 d236f/ 02.12.15-pincus-testimony.pdf.

[141] H.R. 9, §3(b), *adding revised* 35 U.S.C. §285(a).

[142] *Id.*

[143] H.Rept. 113-279, at 21.

[144] *Id.* at 107 (quoting a letter from the American Association for Justice).

[145] S. 632, §101(12).

[146] S. 1137, §7(a).

[147] S. 1137, §7(b), *adding revised* 35 U.S.C. §285(a).

[148] S. 1137 (as reported), §7(b), *adding revised* 35 U.S.C. §285(a).

[149] Ryan Davis, *4 Differences in the House and Senate Patent Troll Bills,* Law360.com, April 30, 2015 (citing the views of several patent litigators).

[150] S. 1137, §7(b), *adding revised* 35 U.S.C. §285(d)(1). However, the PATENT Act would permit a court, in exceptional cases, to award reasonable attorney fees to the prevailing party in a civil action that includes a claim for relief arising under Section 271(e). *Id., adding revised* 35 U.S.C. §285(d)(2).

[151] Fed. R. Civ. P. 19.

[152] Fed. R. Civ. P. 20.

[153] *Id.*

[154] Joint and several liability occurs when two or more people are found liable, and the plaintiff may collect the entire judgment from any one of the parties or from any and all of the parties in various amounts until the judgment is paid in full. *See* Black's Law Dictionary, 2d. ed.

[155] 35 U.S.C. §299(a).

[156] *Id.*

[157] *Id.* §299(b).

[158] The Manager's Amendment to the Innovation Act provided a definition of "substantial interest" to include an interest in the subject matter of a patent at issue if the party: (A) invented the subject matter, or (B) commercially practices or implements or is engaged in research and development in technology in the field of the subject matter. H.R. 9 (as reported), §3(c), *adding new* 35 U.S.C. §299(d)(7).

[159] H.R. 9, §3(c), *adding new* 35 U.S.C. §299(d)(1).

[160] H.R. 9 (as reported), §3(c), *adding new* 35 U.S.C. §299(d)(6)(A)-(C).

[161] This additional exclusion to the "interested party" definition was added by the Manager's Amendment to the Innovation Act. *See* H.R. 9 (as reported), §3(c), *adding new* 35 U.S.C. §299(d)(6)(C)(i).

[162] This clarification to the "right or ability to direct or control the civil action" was added by the Manager's Amendment to the Innovation Act. *See* H.R. 9 (as reported), §3(c), *adding new* 35 U.S.C. §299(d)(6)(C)(iii).

[163] H.R. 9 (as reported), §3(c), *adding new* 35 U.S.C. §299(d)(5).

[164] *Id.*, §3(c), *adding new* 35 U.S.C. §299(d)(4)(A).

[165] *Id.*, §3(c), *adding new* 35 U.S.C. §299(d)(4)(B). The Manager's Amendment to the Innovation Act states that the joinder provision "shall not apply to an action" if the plaintiff files this certification.

[166] H.R. 9, *adding new* 35 U.S.C. §299(d)(2)(A).

[167] *Id., adding new* 35 U.S.C. §299(d)(2)(B)(i).

[168] H.R. 9 (as reported), *adding new* 35 U.S.C. §299(d)(3).

[169] H.R. 9, *adding new* 35 U.S.C. §299(d)(2)(B)(ii).

[170] H.R. 9, §3(b), *adding revised* 35 U.S.C. §285(b).

[171] Hearing on H.R. 3309 Innovation Act Before the House Committee on the Judiciary, Subcommittee on Courts, Intellectual Property, and the Internet, 113th Cong., 1st Sess., (2013) (Statement of Kevin T. Kramer, Vice President and Deputy General Counsel for Intellectual Property, on behalf of Yahoo! Inc.).

[172] *Protecting Small Businesses and Promoting Innovation by Limiting Patent Troll Abuse: Hearing Before the Senate Judiciary Comm.,* 113th Cong., 1st Sess. (2013) (Statement of Philip S. Johnson, Chief Intellectual Property Counsel, Johnson and Johnson).

[173] *The Impact of Abusive Patent Litigation Practices on the American Economy: Hearing Before the Senate Judiciary Comm.,* 114th Cong. 1st Sess. (2015) (Statement of Hans Sauer, Ph.D., Deputy General Counsel for Intellectual Property, on behalf of Biotechnology Industry Organization).

[174] *Id.*

[175] H.Rept. 113-279, p. 109.

[176] *Id.*

[177] S. 1137, §7(b), *adding revised* 35 U.S.C. §285(c)(1)(A).

[178] *Id., adding revised* 35 U.S.C. §285(c)(1)(B).

[179] *Id., adding revised* 35 U.S.C. §285(c)(2)(A),

[180] *Id., adding revised* 35 U.S.C. §285(c)(2)(B), (C), and (D).

[181] This additional exclusion to the "interested party" definition was added by the Manager's Amendment to the PATENT Act, which was approved by the Senate Judiciary Committee. *See* S. 1137 (as reported), §7(b), *adding revised* 35 U.S.C. §285(c)(2)(E).

[182] *Id., adding revised* 35 U.S.C. §285(c)(1)(B).

[183] *Id., adding revised* 35 U.S.C. §285(c)(1)(C).

[184] *Id.*

[185] *Id., adding revised* 35 U.S.C. §285(c)(1)(D).

[186] *Id.*

[187] *Id., adding revised* 35 U.S.C. §285(c)(1)(G).

[188] *Id., adding revised* 35 U.S.C. §285(c)(1)(F).

[189] In re Seagate Technology, 497 F.3d 1360, 1371 (Fed. Cir. 2007).

[190] *Id.* at 1371-72.

[191] H.R. 9, §3.

[192] *Id.*

[193] H.R. 1896, §2, *adding new* 35 U.S.C. §263.

[194] *Id.*

[195] *Id.*

[196] H.R. 1896, §3, *adding new* 35 U.S.C. §264. H.R. 1896, §2 also would require the USPTO to establish a demand letter database that is publicly accessible and searchable.

[197] H.R. 2014.

[198] S. 632.

[199] 15 U.S.C. §45(a)(1).

[200] S. 632, §202.
[201] *Id.*
[202] *Id.*
[203] *Id.* §203.
[204] *Id.* §204.
[205] S. 1137, §9, *adding new* 35 U.S.C. §299D.
[206] *Id.*
[207] *Id.* §8, *adding new* 35 U.S.C. §299C.
[208] S. 1137 (as reported), §8, *adding new* 35 U.S.C. §299C(b)(3).
[209] *See, e.g.,* Brian Fung, "Patent reform advocates are launching a 'super-coalition' to whack patent trolls," Washington Post, January14, 2015.
[210] *Trolling for a Solution: Ending Abusive Patent Demand Letters: Hearing Before the House Energy and Commerce Comm., Subcomm. on Commerce, Manufacturing, and Trade,* 113th Cong. 2d Sess. (2014) (Statement of Mark Chandler, Senior Vice President and Chief Compliance Officer, on behalf of Cisco Systems Incorporated).
[211] *Id.*
[212] Gene Quinn and Steve Brachmann, "Demand Letter Legislation Must be Narrowly Tailored," March 4, 2015, *available at* http://www.ipwatchdog.com/2015/03/04/demand-letter-legislation-must-be-narrowly-tailored/id=55365/.
[213] P.L. 112-29. For more information on this law, *see* CRS Report R42014, *The Leahy-Smith America Invents Act: Innovation Issues*, by John R. Thomas.
[214] 35 U.S.C. §321(b).
[215] *Id.* §321(c).
[216] *Id.* §324(a).
[217] *Id.* §326(a)(11).
[218] *Id.* §311(c).
[219] *Id.* §311(b).
[220] *Id.* §314(a).
[221] *Id.* §315.
[222] *Id.* §315(e).
[223] *Id.* §316(a)(11).
[224] Ryan Davis, *Senate Bill Tips Scales for Patent Owners in AIA Reviews,* Law360.com, June 5, 2015 (describing the surprise of one practitioner that the legislation contains "such substantial changes to AIA reviews that favor patent owners—which will benefit trolls when their patents are challenged—when the rest of the bill appears aimed at aiding infringement defendants.").
[225] USPTO, *Changes to Implement Inter Partes Review Proceedings, Post-Grant Review Proceedings, and Transitional Program for Covered Business Method, 77 Federal Register* 48680 (August 14, 2012) (final rule).
[226] 37 C.F.R. §42.100(b).
[227] In re Cuozzo Speed Technologies LLC, 778 F.3d 1271 (Fed. Cir. 2015).
[228] *Id.* at *16.
[229] *Id.* at *17 (quoting *In re Prater*, 415 F.2d 1393, 1396 (CCPA 1981).
[230] *Id.* at *17.
[231] *Id.* at *21.
[232] H.R. 9, §9, *adding new* 35 U.S.C. §316(a)(14)(A); S. 1137 (as reported), §11(a)(4)(A)(vii).
[233] *Id., adding new* 35 U.S.C. §316(a)(14)(B).
[234] H.R. 3309, *the "Innovation Act:" Hearing Before the House Judiciary Comm., 113th Cong.,* 1st Sess. (2013) (Statement of David J. Kappos, Former Under Secretary of Commerce for Intellectual Property and Director of the United States Patent and Trademark Office), at 8.
[235] *Id.*
[236] Ryan Davis, *Innovation Act Would Revamp AIA Reviews to Shield Patents,* Law360.com, February 10, 2015 (explaining that "[c]onstruing the claims of a patent in an AIA review

broadly means that significantly more prior art can be used to invalidate the patent than would be available in district court. A majority of AIA final decisions to date have invalidated at least some claims of the patent.").

[237] Business Software Alliance (BSA) Letter to Speaker Boehner and Minority Leader Pelosi, July 9, 2015, *available at* ihttp:// www.bsa.org/~/media/ Files/Policy/ SoftwareInnovation/ Letters/07092015InnovationActLetter.pdf, at 1.

[238] Information Technology Industry Council Letter to Senate Judiciary Committee Chairman Grassley and Ranking Member Leahy, June 3, 2015.

[239] 35 U.S.C. §325(e).

[240] H.R. 9, §9(a), *amending* 35 U.S.C. §325(e)(2); S. 1137, §14(a).

[241] *See* Colleen Chien and Eric Goldman, *In its Rush to Fix Patent Reform, Congress Didn't Fix Its Biggest Error,* Forbes.com, January 2, 2013; *see also* 158 Cong.Rec. S8517 (daily ed. December 28, 2012) (statement of Senator Leahy) ("Regrettably, the legislation passed today does not include one technical correction that would improve the law by restoring Congress's intent for the post-grant estoppel provision of the America Invents Act. Chairman Smith recently described certain language contained in that provision as an 'inadvertent scrivener's error.' As written, it unintentionally creates a higher threshold of estoppel than was in the legislation that passed the Senate 95-5, or that was intended by the House, according to Chairman Smith's statement. I hope we will soon address this issue so that the law accurately reflects Congress's intent.").

[242] 35 U.S.C. §§316(e), 326(e).

[243] S. 632, §102(c), *adding revised* 35 U.S.C. §316(e)(1); S. 632, §103(c), *adding revised* 35 U.S.C. §326(e)(1).

[244] *Id.* §102(c), *adding revised* 35 U.S.C. §316(e)(2); S. 632, §103(c), *adding revised* 35 U.S.C. §326(e)(2).

[245] S. 1137 (as reported), §11(a)(4)(C)(ii), *amending* 35 U.S.C. §316(e) (for IPR proceedings); S. 1137 (as reported), §11(b)(4)(C)(ii), *amending* 35 U.S.C. §326(e) (for PGR proceedings).

[246] Information Technology Industry Council Letter to Senate Judiciary Committee Chairman Grassley and Ranking Member Leahy, June 3, 2015.

[247] H.R. 9 (as reported), §9(b)(1), *adding new* 35 U.S.C. §316(a)(15) (regarding IPR); H.R. 9 (as reported), §9(b)(1), *adding new* 35 U.S.C. §326(a)(14) (regarding PGR).

[248] *See* H.R. 9, *the Innovation Act: Hearing Before the House Judiciary Comm.,* 114th Cong., 1st Sess. (2015) (statement of Mr. Hans Sauer, Deputy General Counsel, Biotechnology Industry Organization) (arguing that "the statistically disproportionate 'kill rates' of IPR proceedings invite unintended abuses and predatory practices by those seeking to attack patents for illegitimate reasons, including for their own financial gain ... "); *see also* Joseph Walker and Rob Copeland, *New Hedge Fund Strategy: Dispute the Patent, Short the Stock*, WALL ST. JOURNAL, April 7, 2015 (describing a recent strategy employed by a hedge fund manager, Kyle Bass, in which he files IPR petitions to challenge the validity of patents protecting drugs offered by certain pharmaceutical companies; after filing the IPR, he either shorts the stock of those drug companies (whose stock prices likely fall due to news of the IPR being initiated) or buys shares in other companies that would benefit from the patent being held invalid).

[249] S. 632, §102(d), *adding new* 35 U.S.C. §311(d)(2).

[250] The STRONG Patents Act defines the term "charged with infringement," for purposes of this standing provision, to mean "a real and substantial controversy regarding infringement of a patent exists such that the petitioner would have standing to bring a declaratory judgment action in Federal court." S. 632, §102(d), *adding new* 35 U.S.C. §311(d)(1).

[251] S. 632, §103(d), *adding new* 35 U.S.C. §321(d)(2).

[252] S. 1137 (as reported), §11(a)(2), *adding new* 35 U.S.C. §314(a)(2) (regarding IPR); S. 1137 (as reported), §11(b), *adding new* 35 U.S.C. §324(a)(2) (regarding PGR).

[253] S. 1137 (as reported), §11(c)(1).

[254] *See* Figueroa v. United States, 466 F.3d 1023, 1027-28 (Fed. Cir. 2006). The USPTO became fully user-fee funded as a result of P.L. 101-508, the Omnibus Budget Reconciliation Act (OBRA) of 1990. For more information about USPTO's funding structure, *see* CRS Report RS20906, *U.S. Patent and Trademark Office Appropriations Process: A Brief Explanation*, by Glenn J. McLoughlin.

[255] In the absence of an appropriation making fees collected by an agency available to that agency, the collected fees are placed in the general fund of the Treasury as miscellaneous receipts, unless otherwise directed. *See* Government Accountability Office (GAO), Office of the General Counsel, 3 Principles of Federal Appropriations Law 1-12 (2004) (citing 31 U.S.C. §3302(b)).

[256] *See* Intellectual Property Owners, *USPTO Funding, at* http:// www.ipo.org/ index.php/ advocacy/hot-topics/uspto-funding/.

[257] 35 U.S.C. §42(c)(2).

[258] *Id.*

[259] H.Rept. 113-279, p. 104.

[260] A bill introduced in the House, the Innovation Protection Act (H.R. 1832), would similarly end USPTO fee diversion. However, this legislation does not contain provisions unrelated to the funding of the USPTO.

[261] S. 632, §107(a)(4), *adding revised* 35 U.S.C. §42(d)(2).

[262] *Id.* §107(a)(2), *adding revised* 35 U.S.C. §42(c)(1).

[263] *Id.* §107(a)(4), *adding revised* 35 U.S.C. §42(d)(4).

[264] 28 U.S.C. §1400(b).

[265] VE Holding Corp. v. Johnson Gas Appliance Co., 917 F.2d 1574, 1581 (Fed. Cir. 1990).

[266] *Id.* at 1583.

[267] Ryan Davis, *House Bill Would Shut Down Eastern Texas Patent Docket,* Law360.com, June 12, 2015, *at* http://www.law360.com/articles/667339/house-bill-would-shut-down-eastern-texas-patent-docket (noting that "u]nder current venue rules, nonpracticing entities are able to buy up patents and rent an office in the Eastern District of Texas in order to establish venue there, then have free rein to sue just about any company in America. Given the district's reputation and history of large jury awards for patent owners, many nonpracticing entities take advantage of that opportunity.").

[268] Statement of Chairman Goodlatte, on the Manager's Amendment to the Innovation Act, *available at* http://judiciary.house.gov/index.cfm/hearings?Id=2848E2C2-F705-4A03-800C-64930626A395&Statement_id= CF3D1F76-9219-4E6C-9B28-692BD6206E21.

[269] H.R. 9 (as reported), §3(g)(1), *amending* 28 U.S.C. §1400(b).

[270] H.R. 9, §7(a)(1); S. 1137, §12(a)(1).

[271] *Id.* §7(a)(2); S. 1137, §12(a)(2).

[272] S. 632, §111(c)(1).

[273] *Id.* §111(c)(2).

In: Patent Litigation Reform
Editor: Richard K. Gutierrez
ISBN: 978-1-63485-526-6

Chapter 2

STATEMENT OF MARK GRIFFIN, GENERAL COUNSEL, OVERSTOCK.COM. HEARING ON "PATENT REFORM: PROTECTING AMERICAN INNOVATORS AND JOB CREATORS FROM ABUSIVE PATENT LITIGATION"*

Chairman Goodlatte, Ranking Member Conyers, and Members of the Judiciary Committee, I am Mark Griffin, General Counsel of Overstock.com, Inc. Thank you for the opportunity to testify before you today on behalf of Overstock, and United for Patent Reform, about protecting American innovators and job creators from abusive patent litigation.

ABOUT OUR COMPANY

As the twentieth century drew to a close, online shopping was just beginning to emerge. In early 1999, Dr. Patrick Byrne, the founder of Overstock.com, recognized that the Internet presented the ideal platform for liquidating excess inventory. Until the advent of online retail, smaller businesses had no efficient "close-out" merchandising process, and customers

* This is an edited, reformatted and augmented version of a statement presented March 25, 2015 before the House Judiciary Committee, Subcommittee on Courts, Intellectual Property and the Internet.

looking for bargains had to traipse to brick-and-mortar outlet centers with limited selections. And so, in October of 1999 in Salt Lake City, Utah, with no outside funding and with real innovative vision, Dr. Byrne launched Overstock.com, the premier online business, providing excess inventory to retail consumers at significant savings.

Our website gives customers a simple and convenient way to shop for quality products at the best prices, 24 hours a day -- with a broad selection of more than a million products on the site. We have grown from a handful of employees and suppliers in 1999 to roughly 1,500 employees and over 3,200 suppliers today. We not only deal in discounted, closeout merchandise, but also value-priced brand products of all shapes and sizes, including, furniture, home decor, housewares, bedding and bath, consumer electronics, apparel, jewelry, sporting goods, books, DVDs, and video games. We built our brand on first-rate customer service, and it's paid off: Since 1999 we have grown in revenue from $1.8 million, to $1.3 billion last year. The Overstock.com story exemplifies what is best in the American Innovative Spirit.

About United for Patent Reform

United for Patent Reform is a broad coalition of diverse American businesses who are pursuing comprehensive solutions to abusive patent litigation. Instead of creating new jobs and investing in new technologies, businesses, large and small, across many industries from national realty, construction, auto manufacturers and technology businesses to Main Street retail shops, hotels, grocers, convenience stores, and restaurants, are diverting precious resources to settle with or fight patent trolls.

Our Experience With Patent Assertion Entities

At Overstock.com, we know tech innovation. Dr. Byrne frequently observes that when we started, "We were a lemonade stand, stapled to a small computer; and now we are the opposite: a big computer stapled to a lemonade stand." We thrive on useful, proper innovation. We have to innovate to survive. We are a strong respecter of intellectual property. We own patents ourselves, and we license technologies we need from inventors; we spend a fair amount of our budget each year buying and licensing intellectual property necessary to our operations. Technology and intellectual property are at the center of our business.

But we also know what abuse of innovation is: It is patent trolls trying to extort money from productive and profitable businesses by suing on weak, vague patents, and banking on the notion that so many of their litigation victims will settle rather than defend themselves, because patent litigation defense is brutally expensive. Overstock.com is not one of those victims. We firmly believe that feeding abusive trolls only attracts more trolls. We follow a "spend and defend" strategy -- we would rather pay real dollars in high defense costs than give a dime to abusive patent trolls.

Since 2004 we have been sued 32 times for patent infringement, and we have spent approximately $11 million to defend these actions. Our lawyers are among the most effective in the business, but they are also efficient and economical; I have no doubt that similarly-situated companies elsewhere pay much higher legal defense fees. And so you can see why so many of them do not want to pay high defense costs; in the short run, it is cheaper and less risky to pay the troll to go away. But the trolls never actually go away. We have in our history settled a handful of cases for small values, though our experience in those cases only reinforced our belief that litigating every unjust assertion of patent infringement is the better strategy.

While expensive, our fighting strategy has proved to be a good investment. Three of our cases were dismissed by the courts during pre-trial motion practice. We won a large case in 2011, invalidating the troll's principle patent. As a result of our approach and the fighting reputation we have earned, with increasing frequency, patent trolls simply dismiss their cases against us when they discover that we intend to fight, rather than settle. In the last three years, for example, 12 trolls have dismissed their cases against us—simply walked away with no settlement payment of any kind. When they want us not to publicize the dismissals, we often refuse. We want everyone to know that trolls leave empty handed, without a dime of the money that we would rather spend building our business. As Patrick Byrne said last year, when two of those trolls, Execware and Eclipse, walked away from us empty-handed and a bit bruised: "In abusive lawsuits, we spend our legal budget in defense, not on unjust settlements."

While it is rewarding to see this approach pay dividends for us, many other retailers and others who receive frivolous patent demands cannot afford to spend tens of millions of dollars to scare trolls off the bridge. Moreover, a well-functioning patent system should not impose this kind of tax on innocent operating companies. Congressional action establishing national litigation standards applicable in all federal courts can help to reduce the burden of abusive patent litigation and deter abusive practices, so that each company does not need to individually bear the great expense of standing up against trolls on its own.

Legislative Reform

We have heard about a number of possible reforms to the litigation system that would make it less attractive to trolls. Multi-faceted reform would help cure the economic asymmetries that make their extortionate approach profitable against the many companies that lack the resources and the will to stand up to trolls.

First, we believe it is crucial to raise the pleading standards in patent litigation, to make trolls explain their infringement claims in more detail when they file a complaint. Currently, courts do not require that a patent holder explain how a patent is infringed, or even identify the product involved, which makes it nearly impossible for someone who has been sued to evaluate the case and decide how to respond. Adding to the difficulties of a legitimate company facing such a vague lawsuit, trolls can then demand vast amounts of discovery, which is burdensome and very expensive for the defendant. The trolls then have more leverage to extort a settlement, and companies will often settle a case just to avoid those discovery costs -- without ever really knowing whether the suit had any merit at all. Genuine notice pleading, as we have in other areas of the law, will allow defendants to determine what exactly is alleged to infringe and make an informed decision as to how to best proceed with the case, and it will remove one unfair advantage from the trolls' arsenal.

Second, in patent litigation, we need a pecking-order priority between those who merely use an alleged infringing product and those manufacturers or suppliers from whom the user purchases. Patent trolls often prefer to file suits against end-user customers for a technology these customers purchased, but did not manufacture. It is imperative that that claims of infringement proceed first between a patent owner and a manufacturer, before claims are allowed to proceed between the patent owner and the manufacturer's customers. Under current law, anyone can be sued for infringement for using a product, system or method. We don't want to change that. Instead, it simply makes sense for cases against end-users to be stayed in favor of cases involving the manufacturer. Trolls often pick on users of products rather than manufacturers because users are easier targets—the users, not being the original producer, often lack access to the information to form a proper defense. They may not even know that they are using a patented product, and they likely have less familiarity with the patent litigation system than a manufacturer of patented products does. And trolls not only target users, they often target users that are small businesses, who lack not only the information and experience to take on a patent infringement suit, but the legal staff and financial resources. Besides, as long as trolls can sue users and avoid the manufacturers, they stand to garner many unjust settlements without any real risk of having weak infringement claims vigorously contested.

Third, we need a better discovery process. Patent trolls exploit the discovery process to drive up costs, making settlement the less costly option for a troll target. They make extraordinarily broad claims about a patent's scope, and then make correspondingly extensive claims for very far-reaching discovery. Not only do they put the defendant company to extraordinary costs, but they risk nothing in return, for they make no products and document nothing but their litigation. Legislation should make patent litigation more efficient so that weak cases can be dismissed before too much expensive discovery. For example, requiring patentees to explain, and judges to decide, what a patent means—at the *Markman* hearing—before the majority of discovery would drive early resolutions and avoid unnecessary costs. Indeed, trolls will sometimes drop cases at the *Markman* stage, if their broad and spurious claims are rejected by the judge, and even if they are not, a claim construction before massive discovery will still narrow the issues and focus the case, which promotes quicker and more effective resolutions, often by summary judgment.

Fourth, we need reasonable cost constraints in discovery. For example, trolls should pay for the broad discovery they request, beyond core documents, so that they cannot unjustly ramp defense costs to force settlement. Since trolls don't actually make or create anything, they have few documents to produce. Consequently, most case discovery is one-sided and there is no troll incentive to be reasonable in discovery requests. But only a very few of the thousands of documents routinely produced in troll litigation are ever actually relevant to the dispute, and in today's world of e-discovery and massive record-keeping this all translates to an enormous bludgeon in a troll's hands. Making trolls responsible for the costs of their discovery requests that go beyond the documents needed to decide most patent issues, will stop unreasonable demands made solely for negotiation leverage. And all these decisions could -- and should -- remain squarely within the district court's discretion in managing a case, to ensure that legitimate discovery requests by any party are accommodated.

Lastly, we need better cost-shifting options for judges. Trolls currently have few barriers to litigation with no significant costs. Defendants, on the other hand, face astronomical fees to battle a troll in court: $6 million in legal fees for a large company, and $1 million for a small one, are the cost of doing business in this arena. But trolls face no such risks, and are often set up precisely to be judgment-proof. A stronger fee-shifting statute, and a mechanism to ensure court-ordered fee shifting is enforceable, will strongly deter nuisance suits without any chilling of legitimate suits. Patent law currently allows for fee shifting, and the *Octane Fitness* decision is a helpful step forward in defining "exceptional" cases. It is important, however, that Congress speaks to fee shifting in statute, and give judges better options to deter the rising tide of frivolous troll litigation. Where a suit is truly frivolous, the defendant should be able to seek reimbursement of its reasonable defense costs; no legitimate patent holders need fear such a standard, while the mechanism will surely deter the types of cases trolls routinely file.

AN ESCALATING PROBLEM

Opponents of patent reform claim patent infringement filings are going down, but evidence shows that a record number of patent cases have been filed in recent years. In 2013, that number reached a record high, having increased by 25%.[1] On April 23, 2014, more new patent lawsuits were filed on a single day than on any other day in at least the last 14 years.[2] And so far in 2015, patent lawsuit filing has surged. There were 36% more patent cases filed in January of this year than January of last year[3], and 499 patent litigation cases were filed in February, marking the third straight month-on-month increase in patent lawsuit filing.[4] And to be clear, the alarming majority of these cases are not filed by innovators or owners of patents that they are enforcing in the marketplace; they are filed by trolls, seeking to extract value not by productive use or licensing of patents, but by litigation. Last year, non-practicing entities accounted for 63% of all the patent cases filed.[5] In January of this year, more troll cases were filed than in all of 2004. This is an abuse of the system, and it is escalating. The time is now for meaningful patent reform.

Conclusion

Overstock appreciates Congress' efforts to come to a bipartisan resolution that curbs abuse of the patent system. Considering the significant litigation expenses that Overstock has paid fighting abusive patent litigation, Overstock supports your efforts to help return the rewards of innovation and effort to those who are actually bringing jobs to American workers, and goods to American consumers. The only people who benefit from frivolous patent litigation are the trolls and their lawyers, and that benefit is not enumerated among the original aims of our patent system.

Again, I am honored to have the opportunity today to present our company's experiences which bear on the important questions before you. As you deliberate and discuss the means to fairly adjust the machinery of patent litigation, please remember our voice and the voice of other U.S. retailers. Thank you.

End Notes

[1] Price Waterhouse Coopers, "2014 Patent Litigation Study," July 2014, http://www.pwc.com/us/en/forensic-services/publications/2014-patent-litigation-study.jhtml.

[2] Ryan Davis, "Draft Patent Troll Bill Spurs Huge Spike in New Suits," Law360, May 2, 2014, http://www.law360.com/articles/533893/draft-patent-troll-bill-spurs-huge-spike-in-new-suits.

[3] Lex Machina blog, February 5, 2015, "Patent case trends and the business of litigation."

[4] Michael Loney, "US Patent Litigation Surges in February, Driven by Software Cases," Managing Intellectual Property, March 10, 2015, http://www.managingip.com/Article/3434536/US-patent-litigationsurges-in-February-driven-by-software-cases.html.

[5] RPX Blog on 2014 data, January 9, 2015, "New and Smaller Targets".

In: Patent Litigation Reform
Editor: Richard K. Gutierrez
ISBN: 978-1-63485-526-6

Chapter 3

TESTIMONY OF KATHRYN G. UNDERWOOD, PRESIDENT AND CEO, LEDYARD NATIONAL BANK. HEARING ON "PATENT REFORM: PROTECTING AMERICAN INNOVATORS AND JOB CREATORS FROM ABUSIVE PATENT LITIGATION"*

Chairman Issa, Ranking Member Nadler, and members of the Subcommittee, my name is Kathryn G. Underwood and I am President and CEO of Ledyard National Bank in Norwich, Vermont. I testify today on behalf of the Independent Community Bankers of America and the 6,400 community banks they represent, particularly the hundreds and perhaps thousands of community banks that have received deceptive and abusive demand letters from patent trolls. Thank you for convening this hearing on: "Patent Reform: Protecting American Innovators and Job Creators from Abusive Patent Litigation." I welcome the opportunity to share my bank's experience with an abusive patent troll and to discuss legislative solutions to this problem.

Ledyard is a $434 million asset community bank with seven branches in New Hampshire and Vermont and just over 100 employees. We are primarily a small business lender though we are also active in mortgage and consumer lending. Ledyard is integral to the economic life of the communities we serve.

---

* This is an edited, reformatted and augmented version of testimony presented March 25, 2015 before the House Judiciary Committee, Subcommittee on Courts, Intellectual Property and the Internet.

In September 2011, we received a letter from a patent troll's lawyer informing us that he had filed a complaint against us in the District Court for Vermont. The complaint, which was two inches thick, asserted that our nine ATMs were infringing on his client's patent. However, the troll was willing to settle prior to litigation on "exceptionally favorable terms," if we responded within two weeks. This is a fairly typical "demand letter."

On its face, the claim was absurd. The patent covers the process of connecting an ATM to the Internet. Ledyard's ATMs, being older models, connect to the bank via closed telephone circuits. Infringement was impossible. Though we informed the troll of this fact, through our lawyer, it was of no interest to him. His sole interest was enticing a costly settlement from Ledyard and other community banks.

Identical demand letters were sent to four other New Hampshire banks that day. One settled immediately to avoid the hassle and expense of litigation. Pooling our resources, the remaining four of us jointly assessed the claim, spending hundreds of hours of senior staff time in research and consultations. We contacted the company that provided our ATMs. Wouldn't it make sense for the ATM provider to bear the cost of settlement or litigation? Were they not best positioned to defend against the assertion of infringement? Ledyard is no more than the end-user of the ATM; we didn't develop the technology. Unfortunately, that company assured us that their contracts protected them from an infringement suit against the end-user which limited our options.

Our lawyers advised us that the cost of defending ourselves in patent litigation could be very costly, even if we teamed up with the other banks to reduce costs. Legal bills well in excess of $100,000 could be expected if the case went to trial. Even if we won, that cost could not be recovered unless we could establish the claim was frivolous. The cost to settle was significantly smaller than that. We eventually did settle, but I am not at liberty to disclose the settlement amount. It was a painful decision that no legitimate business person should ever have to face. It violated my basic sense of fairness. On the other hand, I had to consider the best interests of my shareholders, employees, customers, and the communities we serve. I felt it was my duty to view it as a simple economic decision. At the time, we had only an estimate of the cost of litigation; it could have run much higher. Litigation is fraught with risk and uncertainty, even when a case, like ours, seems to be air tight. In addition, litigation would have been months-long or even years-long distraction to me and my management team. The settlement demand, on the other hand, was a known cost; the risk could be monetized and quickly put behind us, allowing us to get back to serving the lending needs of our customers.

Sadly, this is exactly the calculation that the patent troll counted on us making. It's the patent troll business model, and it is especially effective when it is targeted at a small business with limited resources. Community banks are filled with staff dedicated to serving customers and managing risk. In targeting small institutions that may not have a lawyer on staff competent to evaluate the claims, demand letters are sure to reach a captive mass of people afraid of getting sued. Community bank CEOs like me are only too eager to avoid the risk and uncertainty of litigation. Patent trolls practice a legal form of extortion.

In a way, Ledyard is fortunate because this same troll later demanded significantly higher settlement fees from community banks like ours. Undoubtedly, they sought to maximize their returns by seeking the exact price point at which a community bank would choose settlement over litigation. Many community banks chose settlement. Although it violates one's basic sense of right and wrong, paying up makes economic sense for a community bank of my size. Other community banks chose litigation and, I am pleased to say, have been successful. I am unaware of a single instance where this troll has prevailed when it actually went to court. However, despite the court losses, the troll continued to send demand letters to community banks and credit unions, seeking to wring as many settlement dollars as possible from unwitting victims.

The business model of a patent troll stands in stark contrast to the business model of a community bank. We foster long-term relationships with our customers. We are invested, often for generations, in our communities. Our prosperity is linked to their prosperity. A patent troll only profits at the expense of their "customers," who are really victims, and drains valuable resources from the economy. While the troll who targeted us is effectively out of business, the abundance of poor quality patents and opportunistic, unethical trolls, ensure that community banks, credit unions, and other businesses, small and large, will continue to be targeted.

What's the economic impact of the patent troll industry? According to a study by Boston University School of Law, the direct costs associated with patent trolling and often litigation are substantial, totaling an estimated $29 billion in accrued litigation and non-litigation costs in 2011. The study does not capture the significant indirect costs borne by our customers. Unchecked, the problem of demand letters will deter institutions like mine from using new technologies at all. The technologies for which patent demand letters and litigation have become common against community banks include some of the things that make financial services most accessible to consumers and keep us competitive with larger banks – ATMs, online and mobile banking, remote check capture, and check processing, just to name a few. Many institutions will decide these technologies – however much they help their customers – aren't worth the risk. If that happens, consumers lose.

SOLUTIONS

Properly crafted legislation has the potential to significantly curb patent abuse. A number of solutions have been proposed. ICBA recommends that this committee prioritize two solutions in particular that carry the most value in providing relief for community banks.

Demand Letters

Demand letters often lack specific information about the patent, such as what exactly has been infringed, or even the name of the person or entity that owns the patent. With little to go on and a natural aversion to litigation many community banks and credit unions choose to settle.

This Committee can ensure that demand letters contain greater specificity. Enhanced transparency will help curb abusive lawsuits. ICBA supports legislation that would provide that if a demand letter does not contain clear and detailed information about the patent, including the owner of the patent and what has allegedly been infringed, any civil action that is later brought by the troll would be dismissed. Exceptions should be made for legitimate patent holders—specifically, where the primary business of the patent holder is research, development, and manufacturing or selling goods or services. Also, a written communication between parties regarding an existing licensing agreement would not be covered and the court would be able to waive the requirements if it determines that it is in the interest of justice. This is a narrowly targeted solution that does not interfere with the right of any patent holder to send a demand letter.

Covered Business Method (CBM) Program

The American Invents Act created the Covered Business Method (CBM) program, a post-grant review proceeding within the Patent and Trademark

Office (PTO) to re-examine the validity of questionable business method patents. Unfortunately, without intervening action, the CBM program will expire in 2020 once again leaving certain industries exposed to low quality business method patents. The CBM program should be made permanent as it has proven to be a successful low-cost alternative to litigation of covered business method patents. In fact, there are currently several CBM proceedings underway that could benefit banks and credit unions of all sizes.

Additionally, we support language granting the Director of the PTO discretionary authority to waive the filing fee for the CBM program. This provision would be beneficial for smaller financial institutions and could help deter patent trolls from sending abusive and extortive demand letters. It would ensure that institutions of all sizes have access to the CMB program.

End User Indemnification/Warrantee

Community banks often white-label products that are purchased from vendors to serve their customers. As "end-users" of these products and services, community banks should not be on the hook for the infringement claims of trolls.

Community banks are especially vulnerable to the threat of legal action because they lack the resources and market power to fairly negotiate the protections they need when contracting with large sophisticated technology vendors. As was true in my case, the vendors that provide these products and services to community banks often do not stand behind them. As a result, when a community bank is accused of infringement, the vendor, often better situated to refute the claim, sits on the sidelines and refuses to defend their customers. Congress should amend current law to ensure that vendors that sell products or services to community banks provide the appropriate warranties and indemnification to protect the end users from infringement claims.

CONCLUSION

Thank you again for the opportunity to testify today and share my story, which is sadly typical of thousands of community banks and credit unions. Patent trolls represent a significant and growing threat to free commerce and a drain on our nation's economic resources. ICBA strongly encourages this

Committee to take up legislation that includes the recommendations I have described above.

In: Patent Litigation Reform
Editor: Richard K. Gutierrez

ISBN: 978-1-63485-526-6

Chapter 4

STATEMENT OF TODD MOORE, FOUNDER AND CEO, TMSOFT LLC. HEARING ON "PATENT REFORM: PROTECTING AMERICAN INNOVATORS AND JOB CREATORS FROM ABUSIVE PATENT LITIGATION"*

I am Todd Moore, founder of TMSoft LLC, a Virginia-based developer of mobile apps and games. I'm probably best known for creating the White Noise app for your smartphone which help millions of people sleep better at night. My app has been featured on the Dr. Oz show, Today Show, Fox and Friends and more. Jimmy Fallon even made fun of it on his show with a special, not-so-soothing "Axl Rose" edition.

I am a member of CEA, an association representing over 2,000 of America's most innovative companies. CEA also owns and produces the International Consumer Electronics Show every January in Las Vegas. I am also a board member of the Application Developers Alliance ("Apps Alliance"), a non-profit global membership organization that supports developers as creators, innovators, and entrepreneurs.

* This is an edited, reformatted and augmented version of a statement presented March 25, 2015 before the House Judiciary Committee, Subcommittee on Courts, Intellectual Property and the Internet.

Thank you for this opportunity to testify about the importance of the Innovation Act and its critical importance to app developers like me and startup innovators nationwide.

I founded my company in 2008 to create smartphone applications. I worked nights and weekends on different app ideas while keeping a full time job to pay the bills. One of the apps I created, White Noise, started getting a lot of attention in the press and at one point became the #1 app on iTunes. White Noise generated enough revenue so I could quit my job, focus on my startup full-time, and hire employees. I was living the entrepreneurs dream, but I never dreamed the biggest danger to my business would come from a patent troll.

In 2011 my company received a demand letter from Lodsys claiming my app was infringing on one or more of its patents. Lodsys is a privately held "patent monetizing firm" that does not make or produce any products. I was sued in Marshall, Texas - where I have never been but where patent trolls are a local industry that seems to be enabled and supported by local courts.

The demand letter included a screenshot of White Noise showing a webpage inside the app with a button that opened the iTunes App Store - essentially, a hyperlink. I immediately assumed they had simply made a mistake because hyperlinks are universally common technology - in fact, they are the building blocks of the entire World Wide Web. However, I later found out that numerous other app developers had received similar demand letters. Lodsys wanted us all to pay a licensing fee or they would sue for patent infringement.

Lodsys filed a lawsuit against my company and numerous other app developers in 2013. Although the lawsuit was clearly frivolous, I was forced to defend myself and my company in the court system. I was aware that litigation could cost well into the millions of dollars. I knew I didn't have that sort of money - and the patent troll knew that too.

Lodsys was quick to offer me a way out – all I needed to do was wire $3,500 to an overseas bank account and promise never to speak publicly of the case, and they would dismiss the lawsuit.

Most companies would take that deal without hesitation, but many companies that settle with patent trolls risk catching the attention of other patent trolls looking to make quick profit. Another issue with settling is you won't be able to speak publicly about it because the troll demands a non-disclosure agreement that prevents you and your company from speaking about the terms of the settlement. As someone who likes to speak publicly about technology and the software industry, censorship did not sit well with me.

Through the Apps Alliance, I met Dan Ravicher from the Public Patent Foundation, a nonprofit organization whose mission is to represent the public's interest in the patent system. Dan Ravicher agreed to defend my company pro bono. Once Lodsys understood that TMSoft would not roll over and pay an easy settlement and that we had a free lawyer who would challenge the patent's validity, it looked for its own escape. Trolls are not interested in asserting valid patents and obtaining fair royalties; they are interested in easy settlements and quick paydays that fund their next set of lawsuits.

Patent trolls have utterly distorted the patent system. Legitimate licensing of patents allows the exchange of valuable technologies for fair prices so that others can use inventions and build great new products and services. Patent trolls, in contrast, destroy value. I was lucky to have a free patent attorney, who estimates that the several hundred hours his team spent on my case would have cost me $190,000 at a typical patent litigation firm. And we had not yet set foot in a courtroom.

It is likely that the Patent and Trademark Office would have not granted the Lodsys patent under today's new rules. But that future-looking solution is not a complete solution, because the Lodsys patent and thousands of low-quality patents were approved by PTO for 20 years under the old rules, and they are ammunition for patent trolls unless Congress acts.

Also notable is that Apple had already licensed the Lodsys patent from Lodsys, and Apple then provided licensed technology to me. Congress must provide end-user protections to users of software (and not only hardware) so that trolls are required to sue the real alleged infringer, not only small companies like mine that generally are easy marks for quick money. In my case the troll would have been forced to sue Apple, Google or Microsoft - and this troll wasn't looking for that kind of fight.

Ignoring patent trolls and hoping they'll go away is not a solution. The patent troll business model is low-risk and high-reward, as trolls get free contingency-fee lawyers and put their junk patent assets in shell companies. They are destroying small businesses while offering society absolutely no benefit.

My small business has licensed technology and media from many companies, and in return we get something useful that improves our products. That is how legitimate companies use patents to build value and great products. In contrast, with patent trolls, you don't get useful technology that can be used in your product. You get an agreement that they won't sue you. That's not how our patent system is supposed to work.

Finally, I've heard claims that patent reform legislation will harm small inventors. This is nonsense. I risked my capital to build a business and invent great apps. I am not discouraged by reforms that will support legitimate patents, legitimate licensing and legitimate enforcement. I'm a small innovator and what harms me is that the patent system is being exploited by litigation opportunists. The only way to protect true inventors with real patentable inventions is for Congress to reform the system so it works as intended.

What patent trolls are doing to small businesses like mine is simply wrong. We need common sense reforms like the Innovation Act that will force patent trolls to think twice about bringing baseless and frivolous lawsuits. Please shut down the patent troll racket and let small businesses like mine get back to innovating, creating jobs, and building great products that people love.

In: Patent Litigation Reform
Editor: Richard K. Gutierrez

ISBN: 978-1-63485-526-6

Chapter 5

STATEMENT OF BRYAN PATE, CO-FOUNDER AND CEO, ELLIPTIGO INC. HEARING ON "PATENT REFORM: PROTECTING AMERICAN INNOVATORS AND JOB CREATORS FROM ABUSIVE PATENT LITIGATION"*

Chairman Issa, Ranking Member Nadler, and Members of the Subcommittee, thank you for inviting me to appear today to discuss the importance of American innovation and how we can protect it. My name is Bryan Pate. In my career I have served as an officer in the United States Marine Corps, developed new products for a semiconductor equipment company, clerked for a federal judge and worked with a number of Fortune 500 companies as a consultant for McKinsey and Co. I left McKinsey to start the company I now lead and I have been working tirelessly for the past ten years to create and build a new industry right here in the United States.

* This is an edited, reformatted and augmented version of a statement presented March 25, 2015 before the House Judiciary Committee, Subcommittee on Courts, Intellectual Property and the Internet.

ELLIPTIGO

Like many American inventions, ElliptiGO began in a garage as a solution to a problem. In 2005, a lifetime of contact sports and endurance athletics caught up with me and I lost the ability to run for fitness because of hip and knee injuries. I considered cycling, but my experience in triathlon convinced me that bicycle saddles are uncomfortable and that cycling workouts simply take too much time. I started using the elliptical trainer, but found I hated being caged indoors at the gym. It hit me that what I really wanted was a low-impact running device that I could use on the street. I decided to purchase one, only to find that no such device existed.

Surprised and frustrated by that fact, I began to look into running injuries and the size of the potential market for a product like this. Convinced that an outdoor elliptical bicycle would appeal to a large number of people, I called up my friend Brent Teal, a mechanical engineer and fellow Ironman triathlete, to see if he would be interested in developing this kind of a product. A few weeks later we met in a Solana Beach, California coffee shop and drew some rough sketches of the concept on a newspaper. He liked the concept and agreed to do all of the engineering work for free. I agreed to pay for everything we needed to buy. We shook hands and formed a partnership to create the world's first elliptical bicycle.

Brent was already a named inventor on some patents and I was familiar with intellectual property rights, so our first step was to determine whether the idea was already patented. While nobody had ever built or sold an elliptical bicycle before, it turned out that Larry Miller, the man who invented the indoor elliptical trainer back in 1994, already held issued patents in the U.S. and Taiwan on the idea of an outdoor elliptical bicycle. Fortunately, we were able to secure a license to Miller's patents, which enabled us to continue pursuing the project and bring an elliptical bicycle to market.

Over the course of the next few years we raised money from a number of investors, hired our first employees, and partnered with a manufacturer. Then, in 2010, ElliptiGO introduced the world to the first elliptical bicycle. Since then we have sold more than ten thousand ElliptiGO cycles and generated more than $20 million in revenue. We now employ fifteen people at our headquarters in Solana Beach, California, with additional employees in Virginia, Illinois, and New York and we are continuing to grow.

As an entrepreneur, I am by definition a risk taker and an optimist. Few things scare me. However, I am here today because broad changes to the patent system proposed by this committee scare me. Since I learned about the provisions contained in H.R. 9, I have spent a considerable amount time trying to understand how they will impact my business. I am afraid that if H.R. 9 is enacted as written it will have the unintended consequence of hurting American innovators and companies like mine, while perversely protecting unscrupulous foreign competitors.

A strong patent system is vitally important to small businesses and entrepreneurs. Intellectual property-intensive industries alone support $8.1 trillion of the U.S. gross domestic product, generate 27 million jobs, and pay employees over thirty percent more than other industries. Entrepreneurial startups alone are responsible for over twenty percent of gross job creation in the United States. Sweeping changes to the patent system will have major repercussions in these industries, and threaten the innovative ideas and job growth they generate I will discuss each of my concerns in detail, but the bottom line is this: If H.R. 9 was the law in 2005 then ElliptiGO would not exist today, and I'm sure that many other small job creating businesses like ours would not be here either.

As you will see below, my objections to the Innovation Act arise from the impact it will have to the entire start-up ecosystem. It is not just the entrepreneur that is needed to start companies and create jobs. He must be supported by a large group of other people, all of whom are acting in their own best interests. Start-ups are extremely risky endeavors and there aren't many investors, workers, partners and inventors willing to get involved with them because of these risks. My fear is that this bill will shift the risk/reward calculus for these groups to the point where it simply won't make sense to support a start-up that relies on patented innovations. Without enough support from every element of this ecosystem, start-ups cannot get off the ground. Because patent-based technology start-ups are a significant engine of growth for our innovation economy, if they go away then it will have serious repercussions for the country.

I believe any efforts to stop abusive patent litigation must take into account the impacts they could have on the start-up ecosystem. I implore you to avoid instituting solutions that end up doing more harm than good. I fear that H.R. 9 as written will have that result.

STAY PROVISION

The "customer stay" provision of H.R. 9 is one of the most alarming parts of the bill. First, the provision is mislabeled. It should be called the "manufacturer, supplier, seller and end-user stay" because every "party accused of infringing a patent or patents in dispute based on a covered product" is entitled to it equally. This means every foreign manufacturer, every foreign trading company, every domestic manufacturer, and every seller of unauthorized copies of our patented product can stay a litigation that has been filed against them. All they need to do is show that there is a separate litigation underway involving a different party accused of infringing the same patent and that other party "makes or supplies" the infringing product at issue. All of these parties have at least 120 days after the initial pleadings are filed to file their stay motion and the court must grant it if they meet the conditions set forth in the bill, all of which appear to be easy to meet. I believe that the stay begs to be abused by infringers and will have the unintended result of crippling the ability of American businesses to fight manufacturers that copy their patented products and flood U.S. markets with cheap, poor quality knock-offs.

The threat of knock-offs being sold in the U.S. is a serious issue for ElliptiGO. We know of a number of Chinese manufacturers who have replicated our product and are currently advertising it for sale on Alibaba.com and other websites. These knock-offs have not yet made their way to the United States, but it is only a matter of time. When these fake ElliptiGO bikes do make it here, the only defense we will have are our nine issued U.S. patents.

If the stay provision is in effect when these knock-offs hit our shores, then we will be in real trouble. For our product, there could easily be more than a dozen different trading companies sourcing from Chinese factories and feeding that supply into the U.S. through a number of sales channels. As discussed, each of the suppliers in China and the sellers in the U.S. would be entitled to take advantage of the stay provision. Nor is the manufacture of infringing products limited to foreign companies. Companies right here in the United States could easily copy our product as well. So, if the stay is enacted into law, I believe it will expose us to an abuse of the patent system that will prevent us from defending our business against unfair infringement by foreign and domestic actors alike.

Once copies of our patented products hit the market, the sellers will likely ignore our cease and desist letters and force us to undertake the significant time and expense of filing a patent infringement action. In response, a Chinese trading company or U.S. manufacturer will likely file a declaratory judgment action against us, requiring the federal court in our infringement action to stay our case against the seller until the suit against the supplier is resolved. This cycle will likely be repeated multiple times by other parties entitled to a stay, causing an endless delay in our ability to get relief through the courts.

Meanwhile, fake ElliptiGO cycles will continue flooding the market unabated, attracting additional sellers of these products and causing our sales to plummet while our legal expenses continue to mount. Because we cannot compete with cheap knockoffs, at some point we will likely be forced to decide whether to sell our business, cease operations or continue to pursue even more litigation because it is the only means we have available to stop these illegal sales.

Perversely, the stay provision will likely be used to insulate all of these subsequent sellers as well from any suits we file against them, effectively making patent enforcement through the district courts fruitless. While we could file a complaint with the International Trade Commission (ITC) to block the import of infringing cycles, this action will neither prevent the sale of existing cycles in the U.S., nor will it have any impact on domestic suppliers of knock-off ElliptiGOs. So long as there is a stay of litigation against the sellers of infringing products, and manufacturers continue to pop up and sell to retailers, we would likely never get the injunction necessary to stop the sale of infringing knock-offs. This will not only destroy our business and undermine the viability of this industry, but this will also put the public at risk if these products start to fail in the field.

Since we started this company, no one affiliated with it ever expected that we would be left unable to defend it from competitors selling knock-offs of our product. None of us would have gotten involved if we thought that this would end up being the case. Myself, Brent, Larry, all of our investors and all of our employees chose to invest our time, resources, money and skills into making ElliptiGO successful based on the fundamental assumption that we would be able to use the venerable U.S. patent system to defend our company against competitors making and selling products that infringe on our patents. I believe that the customer stay provision will have the perverse result of facilitating the sale of knock-off products here in the U.S and put American innovators at a severe disadvantage in the marketplace.

This is incredibly unfair and I think it will have devastating effects for these innovative American companies, especially small ones. Even if I am wrong about how the situation above will actually play out, I believe that introducing the potential for such abuse by potent and unscrupulous competitors will have a chilling effect on future founders, investors and employees of patent-based start-ups. In any case, there is one thing that I can say for certain: if the customer stay provision was law in 2005 and I knew about it, I would not have started ElliptiGO.

When I headed down this path ten years ago I knew that any mechanical bicycle-like device would be easy to copy and distribute. There's no way I would have left my lucrative career path to take on the risk of starting a company if I didn't believe that I could use patents to stop companies from making and selling copies of my product here in the U.S. For the reasons outlined above, the stay provision would have eliminated this belief and ElliptiGO would not exist today.

FEE SHIFTING AND JOINDER

The fee shifting provision obligates the losing party in a patent infringement suit to prove that its "position and conduct" was "reasonably justified in law and fact or that special circumstances (such as severe economic hardship to a named inventor) make an award unjust." While on its face this provision sounds balanced, in practice, I believe that it will disproportionately and adversely impact small companies like mine.

Patent litigation is complicated and the difference between winning and losing can hinge on a variety of factors, many of which are unpredictable at the outset. Something that appears novel to one trier of fact could be completely obvious to another. Patent enforcement actions can turn on the meaning of one word in a claim and how it is applied to the item at issue. At the time we elect to enforce our intellectual property, we won't have the luxury of being absolutely certain about the validity of our patents, sure of how the courts will construe some of the terminology, or know that we are definitely going to win the case. One thing we will know is that if we lose our case, it will be devastating for our business. That's because we don't have much cash and we aren't profitable. The litigation will be long, very expensive and if we lose, our industry will become much more competitive. The passage of this provision will increase the already high risk litigation poses for us by making patent enforcement actions more expensive if we lose but not changing the reward calculation much if we win.

If we lose, then we will almost certainly have to pay for a mini-trial to determine whether or not our position was reasonable. The provision puts the burden of proof on us, so it is going to cost us much more to prove our case than it will for our competitor to counter our arguments. Moreover, any patent litigation we file will likely be against a large player who will welcome the opportunity to bleed a small competitor of their cash when they have everything to gain and very little to lose. So, the cost of losing a case will go up under this provision even if we prove our case was reasonable. If we fail to meet the burden of proving reasonableness, then our litigation costs will at least double and we will almost certainly have to shut down our company. The provision creates a large shift in the risk of losing a patent litigation and will cost us money at the outset just assessing this new risk when contemplating whether or not to file suit.

If we win, then we'll have the option of seeking fees. However, we're likely only going to sue large players where there is an opportunity to win a huge award in damages. So, if we win, we will likely win big. Whether or not we get to collect attorneys' fees if we win won't meaningfully change the outcome of the case for us. So, this provision makes a very slight change in the reward side of the litigation equation.

In sum, for a small company, this provision creates a large increase in the risk of defending ourselves and only a small increase in the rewards of doing so. As a result, it's going to cause small companies like us to be less willing to enforce their patents. That devalues investments in innovation and makes small companies less likely to succeed. This chills the motivation for starting the company in the first place.

The joinder provision layers on top of the fee shifting provision and creates an even worse situation for start-ups. When attorneys' fees are awarded and the loser doesn't have the resources to pay them, H.R. 9 gives the winning party the right to collect from an "interested party." These interested parties will likely include the founders, senior employees, the licensor of the patent at issue, and any investor with the "ability to influence" the litigation. I believe that this provision will have devastating consequences for technology start-ups. If the joinder and fee shifting rules of H.R. 9 were law in 2005, I am certain we would not have been able to start ElliptiGO.

Small technology companies like ours can't get off the ground without participation from several types of stakeholders: founders, investors, employees, and in our case, a licensor. The joinder provisions are both so broad and so vague that I believe they will expose members from each of these groups to *personal liability* for unpaid legal fees in the event the start-up they support loses a patent lawsuit and is unable to convince the judge that its position was justified.

From 2005 through 2010, when ElliptiGO was in its nascent stages, it simply did not have the cash on hand to pay an opposing party's legal fees if we lost an infringement lawsuit. That is not unusual for a start-up. If our licensor, Larry Miller, thought that there was the slightest chance that he would be held personally liable for these fees if we enforced his patent, there is no way he would have licensed it to us. At the time, we were two guys working out of a garage with no real assets other than a pending patent and a prototype. It would have been too risky to put the potential loss of his house into our hands.

Similarly, many of our early investors helped the company with advice and support. All had the ability to influence something as important as the decision to enforce our patent. If they knew that there was a possibility that they would be on the hook for hundreds of thousands of dollars or even millions of dollars in fees, they would have seriously reconsidered investing in our company. It's one thing to lose $50,000 in an investment. It's another thing to be on the hook personally for over a million dollars in legal fees. That's a huge shift in the risk profile of an already risky investment. There are many safer places to put that money and I doubt we would have landed our initial investors under those conditions.

Finally, one of the first employees we hired had recently earned her MBA from Stanford's Graduate School of Business. She could have worked for any number of great companies. If she knew that one of the many risks of working for ElliptiGO included the potential loss of her house from a failed patent enforcement action, I doubt she would have come onboard.

The bottom line is that without the license from Larry Miller, our initial investor group, or our initial set of employees, ElliptiGO would not have been able to get off the ground. I believe that the joinder provision would have made the already challenging process of finding and convincing these people to support us virtually impossible. The fee shifting and joinder provisions introduce a new, incalculable, and very real risk to each segment of the start-up ecosystem. I fear that if it is made law, then even fewer people will be willing to invest their time, money, skills or ideas into bringing new patentable innovations to market.

Heightened Pleading and Discovery

I will touch briefly on two other provisions of the bill that I think will disproportionately impact small businesses: heightened pleadings and discovery sequencing. H.R. 9 requires patent owners to plead a large amount of specific information in their complaint. This includes, but is not limited to: the specific claims allegedly infringed, an identification of the accused process or product that infringes each claim, the name or model number of every allegedly infringing product or process, or a detailed description thereof, a statement of where each element of each patent claim is contained within the allegedly infringing product or process, and a detailed statement of the nature of the alleged infringer's business. Collecting this information and then paying attorneys to translate it into a detailed complaint will take much more time and cost much more than filing a complaint does now. In fact, it would make filing a complaint to enforce a patent right significantly more onerous than filing a complaint in *any* other type of lawsuit.

More importantly, these added burdens disproportionately impact small companies because they delay the filing process, make enforcing patents more complicated and expensive, and force these companies to incur higher expenses at the beginning of the lawsuit. Moving the cash burden earlier in the process makes it particularly painful for a small company that might have a meritorious case but needs to raise funds in order to pursue a patent litigation. Larger companies with more cash can better handle this added complexity and acceleration of costs, so the adverse impacts of these changes will be felt more by smaller companies.

Finally, limiting initial discovery to matters necessary for claim construction also puts patent holders at a disadvantage against infringing companies. The infringer is in the best position to provide the information about the details of their products so the patent holder can assess to what extent they infringe. In many cases, the patent owner *requires* discovery to learn the details of the infringer's product and business necessary to enforce the patent. Delaying that part of discovery will likely lengthen the overall litigation and make patent enforcement more expensive, riskier and less effective for a patent holder.

THE TOTALITY OF THE PROVISIONS

As you have seen, I have a series of concerns with this bill. I've presented each one individually and I believe each one has a different level of impact on ElliptiGO and companies like it. However, it is particularly concerning that they could all be introduced simultaneously if H.R. 9 passes. Acting together, these provisions will be worse for patent holders than the sum of each individually. For example, the heightened pleading standard will make the customer stay provision even more devastating because it will lengthen the time between the introduction of knock-off products and the filing of the first lawsuit and it will cost more up front to file that lawsuit. Fee shifting adds complexity to the decision to file a lawsuit. Combining it with the joinder provision dramatically raises the stakes for nearly everyone involved in the company. Adding a delayed discovery process on top of that means that it could take a patent holder much longer to realize that his case is a loser and expose him to even more costs if the fees ended up being shifted. So it's not only that each provision is concerning in isolation - they compound on each other to make each one even more concerning.

At the end of the day, I fear that introducing these five new and complex constraints to patent enforcement will scare off the people who make patent-protectable innovation happen. Folks like myself who are risk-taking optimistic innovators with the capability and willingness to take on the challenge of starting a company to introduce a new innovation to the world. Folks like our investors who are willing to invest $25,000 - $100,000 into a "flier" and get behind a passionate team. Folks like our employees who made a bet on us because they want to be a part of changing the world. And folks like Larry Miller - the American tinkerers who spend years working in their garages for no pay but end up conceiving of things like the indoor elliptical trainer that not only become multi-billion dollar industries of their own, but inspire other tinkerers like me to improve upon their ideas with innovations like the elliptical bicycle.

All of us in this ecosystem make a conscious choice to drive these innovations forward. To do so we forego other opportunities. We assess the risks, scope the potential rewards, and make our best decision based primarily on those two factors. A strong patent system lowers our risk and increases our potential reward. Provisions that weaken our patents increase our risk and decrease the reward. Once the rewards no longer outweigh the risks, investors will invest elsewhere, employees will work elsewhere, tinkerers will tinker but take it no further, and entrepreneurs will keep their jobs at large companies instead of breaking out on their own. When that happens, the results will be devastating for innovation in this country.

SOLUTIONS

As discussed above, I support efforts to curb abusive patent litigation. I believe this is a problem Congress and the courts can address together. The Targeting Rogue and Opaque Letters Act (TROL Act) pending in the Energy and Commerce Committee would give the Federal Trade Commission and state attorneys general wider latitude to address abusive demand letters as an unfair trade practice. That action alone would help provide relief to thousands of small businesses like mine who may be forced to submit to the unfair and unfounded demands of patent trolls in order to avoid the costs and risks of going to court.

I also support the Supporting Technology and Research for Our Nation's Growth Patents Act (STRONG Patents Act), introduced this month in the Senate by Senators Coons, Durbin, and Hirono. This legislation achieves the goal of addressing abuses of the patent system by curbing demand letters, bringing pleading requirements in line with other federal cases, ensuring the U.S. Patent and Trademark Office (USPTO) has the resources necessary to issue robust patents and ensuring balance in patent post-grant and *inter partes* review procedures at the USPTO.

While addressing the most abusive behaviors in our patent system, I believe that the STRONG Patents Act does *not* pose a threat to small businesses the way H.R. 9 does. If the STRONG Act were law in 2005, I still would have founded ElliptiGO and I would be confident in our ability to defend against foreign knock-offs and unfair competition today. I hope that both of these bills become law.

Conclusion

I appreciate the effort this committee has put forth to address the problem of abusive patent litigation. I hope my testimony will be helpful in developing legislation that will do that without adversely impacting the precious and unique innovation ecosystem we have managed to develop here in America. Please encourage innovators and entrepreneurs to bring new innovations to market by doing what you can to reduce the risks and increase the rewards for innovation. Conversely, please avoid passing legislation that makes it riskier and less rewarding to innovate in this country. Because I believe that the provisions of H.R. 9 will do more harm than good to our economy, I strongly urge you not to pass it.

Thank you for providing me the opportunity to testify before you. I very much look forward to answering your questions.

In: Patent Litigation Reform
Editor: Richard K. Gutierrez

ISBN: 978-1-63485-526-6

Chapter 6

TESTIMONY OF HANS SAUER, DEPUTY GENERAL COUNSEL FOR INTELLECTUAL PROPERTY, BIOTECHNOLOGY INDUSTRY ASSOCIATION. HEARING ON "THE IMPACT OF ABUSIVE PATENT LITIGATION PRACTICES ON THE AMERICAN ECONOMY"*

SUMMARY OF TESTIMONY

As Congress considers legislation to curb misuse of the patent system by entities that seek to use the system for financial gain rather than to promote innovation, Congress must ensure that responsible patent owners remain able to protect and enforce their patents and protect their own businesses against patent infringement. And, in scrutinizing dubious practices of some patent holders, Congress should not overlook abuses by others who seek to undermine the patent system for similarly illegitimate reasons.

Unfortunately, misuse of the patent system against legitimate patent owners is a real and growing problem. In particular, the PTO's Inter Partes Review (IPR) system – a new administrative patent challenge system created by the America Invents Act of 2011 – is undermining the value and

---

* This is an edited, reformatted and augmented version of testimony presented March 18, 2015 before the Senate Judiciary Committee.

predictability of patent rights and wreaking havoc on the legitimate, investment-backed expectations of patent owners. This is happening because, contrary to the intentions of Congress, this new system unfairly stacks the deck against patent owners in many ways, leading to patent invalidation rates far exceeding those seen in district court patent litigation involving similar types of patents and similar grounds for challenges. Not surprisingly, the statistically disproportionate "kill rates" of IPR proceedings invite unintended abuses and predatory practices by those seeking to attack patents for illegitimate reasons, including for their own financial gain. For example, questionable entities have begun to approach biotech companies with threats of dragging their key patents into IPR proceedings unless substantial payments are made. And just recently, the New York Times reported on an investment scheme in which a hedge fund takes a "short" position in the stock of biopharmaceutical companies and then files IPR challenges against one or more patents protecting their key products in an effort to profit from driving down the companies' stock prices. The biotechnology industry is particularly vulnerable to such manipulation, because our companies tend to be small, derive most of their revenue from one or two products on the market, and have just a handful of very valuable patents protecting those products. The mere filing of an IPR demonstrably can have significant impact on the stock prices of such companies, as well as their ability to continue to raise the investment needed to develop future treatments for patients in need. Indeed, the first company to be targeted by this hedge fund strategy was a small biotech company whose main product is an innovative treatment that helps patients with Multiple Sclerosis walk better. In one day this company lost more than $150 million in market capitalization because a hedge fund, which may have shorted the stock, announced an IPR challenge. These market-manipulating, cynical efforts not only damage the value of companies working on cures, but also hurt patients and their families who are eagerly waiting for such cures.

Senators Coons, Durbin and Hirono have introduced the STRONG Patents Act, which BIO supports, which would prevent such abuse.

BIO encourages this Committee to develop a legislative package that will curb abusive patent practices, including the abuse of the IPR system, through a balanced and targeted approach that does not undermine the ability of legitimate patent owners to defend their inventions and businesses against infringement. We believe consensus can be achieved on a range of issues, including enhancing transparency of patent ownership and enforcement; curtailing unfair or deceptive practices in the indiscriminate sending of patent licensing or settlement demand letters; addressing how patents can be enforced against innocent end-users or consumers of infringing products manufactured and sold by others; and making the IPR system a more balanced and fair system for patent owners.

We remain concerned, however, that proposals for more general patent litigation changes presently lack this requisite balance. Concepts such as excessive pleading requirements, mandatory stays of merits discovery, and joinder of third parties as unwilling co-plaintiffs for the purpose of expanding liability for attorney fee awards, are found in no other area of civil litigation and go too far in restricting the ability of all patent owners to enforce their patents against infringers.

The re-introduction of the Innovation Act (H.R. 9) in the House of Representatives revives, on a dramatically shifted landscape, this debate over the right "balance" that was begun in the last Congress. A series of court decisions, Judicial Conference rule changes, PTO actions, and legislative and enforcement activities over the past two years have greatly changed the dynamic for systemic patent litigation reforms – by raising patentability standards and the requirements for filing patent lawsuits; increasing the shifting of litigation costs for baseless infringement suits; reducing the asymmetries in litigation that some plaintiffs have exploited to demand unfair settlements; and enhancing consumer protections against the bad faith assertion of patents against consumers and other end users. In short, both the bar and the stakes have been raised in the patent system, and the result has been a substantial decline in patent litigation since this Committee last considered the need for broad patent litigation reforms. These changes reinforce the need to ensure that any patent reform legislative package does not swing the pendulum too far in any one direction.

Achieving this balance is essential for biotechnology. Reliable patents are critical in ensuring the steady stream of investment necessary to develop innovative medicines, alternative sources of domestic renewable energy, and more productive and sustainable farming techniques that raise farm incomes and reduce environmental degradation. And they are essential to the technology transfer process that leads from inventions in the lab to products on the shelves. A recent independent study pegged the value of such technology transfer to the U.S. economy at up to $1.18 trillion since 1996 alone.

The majority of biotechnology companies are small businesses that have no products on the market, and thus their research and development activities are funded through massive amounts of private sector investment – on average, more than $2 billion per new biotech medicine – which must be sustained over many years, sometimes even decades. Without strong, predictable and enforceable patent protections, many investors will stop investing in biotech innovation or limit such investment to only "low risk" products. This decline in investment will degrade our ability to provide solutions to the most pressing medical, agricultural, industrial and environmental challenges faced by our Nation today.

We look forward to working with this Committee towards developing a balanced legislative package that meets these requirements. We are optimistic that targeted solutions that address the practices of entities who unfairly enforce, or unfairly attack, patents can be achieved.

INTRODUCTION

Chairman Grassley, ranking member Mr. Leahy, members of the Judiciary Committee, thank you for inviting me today to testify on the subject of protecting small businesses and promoting innovation through further patent reform.

By way of personal introduction, I am Deputy General Counsel for Intellectual Property for the Biotechnology Industry Organization, a major trade association representing over 1,100 biotechnology companies, research institutions, technology incubators, and similar entities in the medical, agricultural, environmental and industrial biotechnology sectors. At BIO I advise the organization's board of directors and BIO's various policy departments on patent and other intellectual property-related matters. Prior to joining BIO in 2006, I was Chief Patent Counsel for MGI Pharma, Inc., in Bloomington, MN. I have 20 years of professional in-house experience in the biotechnology industry, having begun my career as a postdoctoral research fellow at Genentech, Inc. in South San Francisco in 1995, and subsequently worked as a research scientist at Guilford Pharmaceuticals Inc. in Baltimore. My research specialty was the biology of age-related degenerative brain disorders; in this role I participated in several drug development programs before becoming a patent lawyer in 2003. I hold an M.S. degree in biology from the University of Ulm in Germany; a Ph.D. in Neuroscience from the University of Lund, Sweden; and a J.D. degree from Georgetown University Law Center where I serve as adjunct professor of law.

BACKGROUND

Very few sectors of the Nation's economy are as dependent on predictable, enforceable patent rights as is the biotechnology industry. Robust patents that cannot be easily circumvented, and that can be predictably enforced against infringers, enable biotechnology companies to secure the enormous financial resources needed to advance biotechnology products to the marketplace, and to engage in the partnering and technology transfer that is necessary to translate basic scientific discoveries into real-world solutions for disease, pollution, and hunger.

Research and development within the biotechnology industry comes at a very high cost, and every idea that is funded comes with a much greater risk of failure than success. Investment thus is predicated on an expected return in the form of patent-protected products or services that ultimately reach the market. The typical BIO member company does not have a product on the market yet, nor a steady source of revenue, and spends tens of millions of dollars on R&D annually. The biotechnology industry as a whole is responsible for well more than 20 billion dollars of annual research investment, and provides employment to millions of individuals nationwide. Virtually all of this investment is through private funding.[1] Developing a single therapy requires an average investment ranging from $1.2 billion to over $2 billion, and the clinical testing period alone consumes more than 8 years on average.[2]

Such investments are not only expensive; they are risky. For every successful biopharmaceutical product, thousands of candidates are designed, screened, and rejected after significant investments have been made. The chances that a biopharmaceutical medicine will advance from the laboratory bench to the hospital bedside are approximately one in 5,000.[3] Only a small minority of candidate drugs even advance to human clinical trials, and most of those will never ultimately reach the market. For example, at the time human clinical testing begins, the odds that a biopharmaceutical compound will eventually receive FDA approval are less than one-third.[4]

Because such risks and costs cannot usually be borne by any one entity alone, biotech drug development depends heavily on licensing, partnering, and access to capital. Patents allow biotech inventions of great societal value to be passed or shared among parties best suited to unlock their potential at any given stage of development and commercialization – each contributing their part, each sharing the risk of failure, each increasing the odds that a product eventually reaches patients.

If these patents can be invalidated under overly broad criteria, or if the ability to enforce them becomes limited due to an exceedingly high bar to filing a lawsuit or excessive delays in prosecuting a case through the courts, third parties would be less likely to invest in or license the technology, and major sources of R&D funding would move elsewhere. The result – patients waiting for the next new cure or treatment will have to wait longer, or may not ever get it at all.

For these reasons, currently-pending patent litigation reform legislation is highly relevant to the biotech business model. A small or mid-sized biotech company that today decides to begin development of, for example, an Alzheimer's treatment must look a decade or more into the future. Long-term financial commitments will be required; several hundred million dollars will need to be raised; and development partnerships will need to be secured in a situation where the cost of capital is high and the odds of ultimate success are small. Because investment-intensive businesses can tolerate only so much risk, even moderate additional uncertainty can cause business decisions to tip against developing a high-risk, but potentially highly-beneficial, product. This is not an academic consideration. Every biotech executive has stories to tell about promising experimental compounds that had very favorable medicinal properties, but were never developed because their patent protection was too uncertain. And scholars have documented this unfortunate fact. [5] The injection of additional systemic uncertainty by, for example, making the enforceability of patents against infringers more uncertain can negatively affect which new cures and treatments may become available a decade from now.

The average American today can realistically hope to live into her or his 8th decade. At retirement, one out of five Americans can expect to develop Alzheimer's disease during her or his remaining years. The risk of developing cancer is even greater. While much has been said about inefficiencies in the patent system that drive up business costs and prices for consumers in some sectors today, we must keep in mind that that same patent system encourages risk-taking and long-term investment in potential solutions for the biggest problems facing our world and the generations to come: disease, hunger, and pollution. Great care must be taken to ensure that we do not focus too heavily on current complaints about abuses in the patent system without appreciating the system's longer-term benefits to society.

In this regard, it is important that, despite strident rhetoric, we do not overlook a 2013 nonpartisan Government Accountability Office (GAO) report[6] that found that patent assertion entities – the so-called "patent trolls" – bring less than 20 percent of patent litigation cases, while traditional businesses bring 68 percent of patent litigation. Any solutions proposed by this Congress must not impede the vast majority of patent owners from trying to enforce their legitimate patents in a legitimate way.

It also is important for Congress to recognize and consider that our patent system is undergoing a period of great change as a result of recent decisions of the courts and the Judicial Conference, the ongoing implementation of major patent legislation enacted only a few years ago, and new challenges posed by emerging technologies. In the barely 16 months since the U.S. House of Representatives voted on the 2013 Innovation Act (H.R. 3309, 113th Congress; passed December 5, 2013), the courts and the PTO have changed the patent litigation landscape in ways that should be carefully taken into account by this Committee. Form pleadings for patent infringement suits will be abolished, thereby heightening and conforming pleading requirements in patent cases to other civil litigation. Discovery in patent litigation will follow a proportionality standard that makes discovery more focused and affordable for both parties, and which will allow the costs of discovery to be shifted to the party seeking it in certain instances. Supreme Court decisions on patent-eligible subject matter and claim definiteness have raised the standard for assessing the validity of patent claims, especially software and business method claims, and have made it easier to invalidate indefinite and/or overbroad patents. Attorney fee awards are allowed more frequently and flexibly in patent cases in the wake of Supreme Court and Federal Circuit decisions, raising the stakes for those who file frivolous or baseless patent suits. Deceptive practices in sending patent demand letters to small businesses are being targeted by the Federal Trade Commission (FTC), state Attorneys General (AGs), and dozens of recently-enacted state laws that clarify consumer protections against phony patent threats.

As a result of these and other developments, the number of patent cases filed has fallen significantly. For example, in comparing the number of new patent complaints filed in September 2013 versus September 2014, the number of new patent infringement complaints decreased by a remarkable 40 percent.[7] 2014 as a whole was down 18% from the previous year, and this decrease so far seems to hold steady.[8]

In parallel, it has become clear that the PTO's Inter Partes Review (IPR) system of administrative patent challenges is having a game-changing effect on the patent litigation system. Patents that are involved in district court litigation are now routinely subjected to "second rail" administrative litigation in the PTO, where they are being invalidated at rates so high that the basic procedural fairness of these proceedings is increasingly being questioned.

It is critical that the future path of our patent system is one that preserves and maintains the incentives for innovation that have made the United States the global leader in medical, agricultural, industrial and environmental biotechnology. With this in mind, I would like to provide the following views on legislation currently under consideration.

DISCUSSION OF LEGISLATIVE PROPOSALS CURRENTLY UNDER CONSIDERATION

At the outset, BIO's member companies reiterate their support for targeted reforms that curtail abusive practices within the patent system, without undermining the ability of patent owners to fairly defend their businesses against patent infringement. We believe it is appropriate for Congress to explore how it can help improve aspects of the patent litigation system, and during the last Congress, BIO and its members invested an enormous amount of effort towards crafting good faith, constructive proposals in this regard, including with the Members and staff of this Committee.

Based on that experience, we believe consensus can be achieved on a range of proposals that were and are being advanced in Congress, including enhancing transparency of patent ownership and enforcement; curtailing unfair or deceptive practices in the indiscriminate sending of patent licensing or settlement demand letters; and addressing the enforcement of patents against blameless end-users or consumers of infringing products manufactured and sold by others. Such provisions would seem to address the most stridently-voiced concerns in the current debate, and would be appropriately focused on the need to protect small businesses, end-users, and others who do not have the resources or the means to defend themselves from unfair or misdirected patent enforcement efforts by dubious patent assertion entities.

To this end, BIO believes that a number of productive proposals have been circulated that deserve this Committee's consideration. For example, the STRONG Patents Act, as recently introduced by Senators Coons, Durbin, and Hirono, contains patent demand letter provisions that should prove effective at protecting small businesses from abusive patent enforcement practices, while at the same time sustaining the ability of innovators to continue to send legitimate licensing and enforcement-related communications to those using their technologies. The "Targeting Rogue and Opaque Letters Act" (TROL Act), a consensus bill that was crafted by the House Energy and Commerce

Committee during the last Congress with diverse stakeholder input, contained similar provisions that were likewise aimed at curbing abusive patent demand practices. As did S. 1720, which as introduced by Senators Leahy and Lee in the past Congress similarly would have brought the indiscriminate, widespread sending of bad-faith demand letters within the ambit of the FTC's enforcement authority. This bill also would have advanced transparency of patent enforcement in litigation by leveraging familiar "interested party" disclosure obligations that already are in use under certain local court rules, and would have provided for "customer stays" that would make it easier for willing manufacturers of allegedly infringing products to join infringement suits against resellers or end-users of their products,[9] thereby providing their customers with relief from litigation pressure.

In contrast to such targeted proposals, other proposals under consideration in the recent and current Congress include far-reaching patent litigation changes, such as:

- New requirements under which initial complaints in patent lawsuits would be required to set forth vastly increased amounts of detailed information or be deemed insufficient and subject to motions to dismiss;
- Mandatory stays of discovery pending patent claim construction, forcing delays of 12 or more months in the typical patent litigation;
- Mandatory stays of actions against a broadly defined class of "customers" that could allow product manufacturers to deflect patent lawsuits towards their suppliers; and
- New impleader authority under which additional parties with a financial interest in the plaintiff or patent at issue – such as investors, licensors, or commercial partners – could be joined to the litigation as unwilling co-plaintiffs to pay the other side's costs under a new "losers pay" approach.

These provisions represent stark departures from the normal civil litigation rules that apply to other commercial litigation under the U.S. system. Congress should consider carefully the wisdom of singling out patent litigation for such an astonishing array of special rules found in no other area of civil litigation. Furthermore, in their current form these litigation reform provisions are one-sided (that is, similar requirements are not imposed on those accused of patent infringement), and will almost uniformly work against patentees of all stripes. In an effort to erect barriers against patent-asserting entities, or so-called "patent trolls," these provisions would systematically raise the cost and risk of patent enforcement for all patentees, with disproportionately greater negative impact on smaller, poorly-funded patent holders.

In this regard, it is important to emphasize that litigation reform, by its very nature, most benefits those who have the means and the will to litigate. In our opinion, large businesses with well-funded litigation budgets are most likely to leverage these litigation changes to their advantage. At the same time, it is questionable whether small businesses that need protection from unfair patent enforcement would be able to leverage sophisticated new litigation maneuvers – such as impleader practice and extensive preliminary motion practice – that would be enabled by the various pending litigation change proposals. Patent litigation is already known as a "game of kings" and surely the pending litigation reform proposals would make it even more so.

The risk of unintended negative consequences on small-business innovation can be illustrated by consideration of several specific pending legislative proposals:

Enhanced Pleading Requirements

H.R. 9 (the Innovation Act) would require that complaints, and counter- or cross-claims, for patent infringement include a number of new information items in order to qualify as legally sufficient. The level of required detail is high and would require plaintiffs to fill out a potentially very large matrix of information: each asserted patent; each claim for each patent; each accused product for each claim; for each accused product an explanation of how each element of each claim meets each feature of each accused product, and the like.

Nobody would disagree that the pleading requirements in patent cases should be enhanced to conform to the standards generally applicable in civil litigation, and BIO supports the proposed repeal of Form 18 in the Federal Rules. However, the proposed exhaustive pleading standard requires an amount of information and degree of specificity that go beyond what would be necessary to support a civil claimant's request for relief and to provide the defendant fair and reasonable notice of the infringement allegation. To legislate pleading requirements at such a high level of specificity invites litigation over the sufficiency of the patentee's efforts even in instances where all parties and the court would agree that there is "enough" for a lawsuit, and where the parties fully understand the factual basis for the infringement allegations. Instead of streamlining the litigation process, the proposed pleadings provision of the Innovation Act would enable accused infringers to litigate whether otherwise sufficient pleading-stage information was nevertheless incomplete; would fuel disputes over whether information was or was not readily accessible and whether the patentee tried hard enough to obtain it; and would empower well-funded defendants to engage in extensive motion practice and "churn" to prevent the litigation from advancing to even its preliminary stages.

The provisions also lack balance and reciprocity: responsive pleadings by alleged infringers often contain counterclaims and affirmative defenses (such as patent invalidity or unenforceability) that frequently fail to provide sufficient notice to the other party (the patentee) of the underlying factual bases for such assertions. But this practice by alleged infringers would not be addressed under the provisions of H.R. 9; only patentees are singled out for additional, burdensome requirements.

We trust that this Committee will understand that patentees do not always have access to the information needed to plead at the outset of a lawsuit, with the required specificity, how the accused infringer's conduct precisely infringes which element of which patent claim. This consideration is particularly relevant to biotechnology, where, for example, a competitor's sophisticated biomanufacturing process, or the use of precursor molecules or proprietary production cell lines, are simply not accessible to a patent owner without some discovery, even if there is good reason to believe that a patent is being infringed.

Accordingly, BIO's members do not believe that such high levels of additional pleading specificity offer a targeted solution that would protect small businesses from abusive patent assertion on the one hand, while at the same time enabling them to protect their own businesses against patent infringement on the other hand. To be sure, some additional information beyond what is currently required under Form 18 of the Federal Rules of Civil Procedure may be beneficial for inclusion in model complaints for patent infringement, so as to convey reasonably detailed information on which the infringement allegation is based. The level of detail should be adequate to allow parties and judges to decide whether there is a sufficient basis for a lawsuit. Indeed, if the complaint sets forth sufficiently detailed grounds explaining why and how at least one patent claim is believed to be infringed, then good grounds for a lawsuit exist. There is no need to additionally require the inclusion within the initial complaint itself of dozens of alternative grounds, or to litigate the sufficiency of such alternative grounds, when it is already clear that there is “enough” for a lawsuit to proceed. To require otherwise would impose an undue burden on the patent owner to plead all details of its case before any discovery has commenced. And doing so would significantly raise the cost and complexity of preparing a patent suit, particularly harming the ability of small businesses to enforce their patent rights, as well as those that need to protect their inventions against competitive threats in an immediate manner.

Instead of legislating this extreme heightened pleading proposal, it would be preferable to amend the law in ways that ensure that the judiciary would play a greater role, and assume more responsibility, for developing the applicable pleading standards in a balanced manner, as part of its traditional rulemaking function. Any final approach also would need to ensure that existing statutory schemes governing certain biopharmaceutical patent litigation are not covered by these new pleading rules, in order to avoid conflicts with the highly detailed nature of the statutory rules already in place for such litigation.

Fee Awards and “Interested Parties”

Within the context of the currently-pending H.R. 9, and the Patent Abuse Reduction Act (S. 1013) from the last Congress, the concepts of “real party in interest,” “loser pays,” and “impleader” are all connected, and should be evaluated together. The cost award and recovery provisions of both bills constitute a true “loser pays” system: as a default, the non-prevailing party must pay the winner’s reasonable costs and expenses, and the burden will be on the loser to explain why it should not have to pay. Under H.R. 9, the non-prevailing party can meet this burden by a showing of special circumstances making an award unjust, or by showing that its position was “reasonably justified in law and in fact.” Among its proponents there is an assumption that this standard will be easy to meet, and that fee and cost awards will therefore occur only in truly frivolous cases. In the same vein, it has been said that this standard is not unprecedented – it is the same standard that has been in place since 1980 in the Federal Equal Access to Justice Act (FEAJA).

Despite such assurances, there is reason to wonder whether cost and fee awards would not occur more often than expected if this standard were transposed to patent litigation.[10] At a minimum, its predicted operation is unclear: unlike many other tort cases, patent cases often do not have clear winners and losers; each party may prevail on some issues and lose on others,[11] such that little can be predicted at this time about how fee awards would be assessed under such a system.

To be clear, BIO's members hold a diversity of views on the advisability of including fee-shifting provisions, such as those of H.R. 9, in any further patent legislation, and therefore BIO does not support or oppose any particular fee-shifting proposal at this time.

Our members have pointed out, however, that proposed "loser pays" provisions currently use overly broad language in defining the classes of civil actions to which they would apply, and are in no way limited to patent infringement actions under title 35 or section 337 investigations in the International Trade Commission under title 19. For example, by their plain terms the provisions include claimants who neither enforce, attack, nor defend against patents – such as a disappointed patent applicant who appeals to a court from an adverse decision of the PTO, or an academic inventor who seeks an accounting of royalties from a non-profit university under the Bayh-Dole Act. Much litigation over the applicability of the provision could, and should, be avoided by narrower legislative language.

In addition, under H.R. 9's fee-shifting provision, patentees (but not defendant-counterclaimants) would be penalized for extending a covenant not to sue after an answer has been filed in the lawsuit, by deeming such a patentee to be a non-prevailing party for purposes of recovering the defendant's attorney fees and costs. Doing so would create disincentives for the private resolution of patent litigation. There also are many legitimate reasons why either party to a patent infringement case may extend a covenant not to sue at some point in the litigation. It remains unclear why covenants not to sue should be disfavored in such a blanket fashion.

We also trust that this Committee is conscious of significant judicial developments in the fee-shifting area, which have taken place over the past year. Federal courts have long had the power to award attorney fees to prevailing parties in exceptional cases, although traditionally the showing required to make a case exceptional has been high, and fee shifting has been uncommon. The 2014 Supreme Court decisions in *Octane Fitness v. Icon* and *Highmark v. Allcare* now permit courts to grant such awards more readily, and provide that a court's fee-shifting decision is reviewed more deferentially on appeal. Preliminary indications are that these decisions may be having a real impact. A recently-published analysis[12] reports 43 published decisions on fee awards in the eight months following the Supreme Court decisions, of which 21 of them, or nearly half, granted a fee award. In contrast, in the eight months *before* the Supreme Court decisions, there were 31 such decisions and only six of them granted fee awards, or less than 20 percent.

The fee-shifting provisions of H.R. 9 also are relevant to the provisions regarding disclosure and joinder of “interested parties.” Under the bill, an interested party would be defined as anyone who has an ownership interest in the patent, or is an exclusive licensee, has enforcement rights, or who has a direct financial interest in the outcome of the litigation, including a right to receive royalties based on the patent or part of a damages award. Under H.R. 9, such “interested parties” must be disclosed in patent litigation, and can be impleaded into the lawsuit and held liable for the winning party's costs, expenses and attorney fees if a fee award is granted.

There is nothing remarkable about the proposition that litigants should identify to the court those who have a financial interest in the litigation or the litigated assets. Under many local court rules, judges require such information today, as they need to know when to recuse themselves from a case, or to take other action to avoid conflicts of interest. But there is a real question whether the pending “real party in interest” provisions go too far in requiring disclosure of any financial interest, including for example, extensive disclosures of patent ownership transfers between subsidiaries having the same corporate parent, and extensive disclosures of third parties having “financial interests” (including passive financial interests) and *their* corporate parents. This level of disclosure would significantly increase the burden of compliance and create traps for unwary legitimate patent holders without providing substantially more useful information in many cases. And, such requirements become particularly problematic when they are being leveraged to join third parties into the lawsuit as unwilling plaintiffs, or to subject them to liability for litigation conduct that is beyond their control.

To this end, H.R. 9 would provide new impleader authority under which the court “shall” grant a defendant’s motion to join “interested” third parties as plaintiffs. These impleader provisions are closely linked to the bill’s litigation cost-shifting provisions, and are intended to ensure that somebody will be responsible for paying the winning party’s litigation expenses if the losing party cannot or will not pay. Only winning defendants would have an opportunity for 3rd party reimbursement, as there are no comparable provisions under which winning patentees can join potential payors on the defendant’s side.

Section 3(c) of H.R. 9 is not the first time impleader practice in patent cases that is being discussed. During the last Congress, H.R. 3309 and S. 1013 contained similar provisions for joining third parties as plaintiffs to ongoing infringement litigation. To inform the Committee's deliberations on the matter, it is useful to highlight some differences between the impleader provisions of these bills: S. 1013 would have provided that the defending party could at any time join an interested party by showing that the plaintiff's interest in "any patent identified in the complaint, including a claim asserted in the complaint, is limited primarily to asserting any such patent claim in litigation." While this definition was intended to capture only "patent troll" lawsuits, BIO was concerned that it could easily apply also to conventional litigation between brick-and-mortar businesses.[13]

The business ramifications of joining unwilling "interested" third parties as co-plaintiffs on the patentee's side of a lawsuit would be significant. As described above, S. 1013 would have defined an interested party as anyone who has an ownership interest in the asserted patent, is an assignee, or an exclusive licensee, or who has a direct financial interest in the outcome of the litigation, including the right to receive proceeds from the litigation. Under this definition, university licensors or business partners who sublicensed the patent to the plaintiff could be impleaded into the litigation at the infringer's option, and face potential liability for the defendant's litigation costs. While university-licensors today often appear as co-plaintiffs in patent cases *pro forma*, the prospect of potentially having to pay part or all of the infringer's defense costs is an entirely new proposition for academic institutions. This is especially problematic when the university-licensor, as is common, does not actually have control over the litigation.

Because they would face potential liability for the patentee's litigation decisions, impleaded university-patent owners or corporate licensors likely would have to hire their own legal teams to participate in the litigation, complicating and raising the costs of patent litigation for all parties. Existing and future licensing agreements would need to be restructured to insulate licensors or business partners from potential liability in these circumstances, or to provide for indemnification. The more risk-averse parties to patent licensing agreements would want to retain enforcement rights or the right to veto patent enforcement decisions and litigation strategies – or worse, may decide against entering into these transactions at all.

The process by which "loser pays" awards can be recovered from third parties under H.R. 9 differs from that described above for S. 1013. First, under section 4 of H.R. 9, the plaintiff must disclose the identity of "interested parties" at the inception of the litigation. Then, the defendant can provide these interested parties notice that they could be impleaded and that the defendant's litigation expenses could be recovered from them if the court confirms that they are an interested party. The third-party recipient of such a notice then has the option to renounce, within 30 days, any and all ownership, right, or direct financial interest in the patent – or otherwise face the risk of being joined to the action at the end to pay the winner's bills. Later, if the plaintiff loses and is subjected to a "loser pays" award that it cannot satisfy, the prevailing defendant can make a showing that the plaintiff had "no substantial interest in the subject matter at issue other than asserting such patent claim in litigation." If this showing is met, the court "shall" grant a motion to implead the third party that was earlier notified. The award can then be made recoverable against the impleaded interested party.

The impleader provision of H.R. 9 is byzantine, and problematic for several reasons. A third party would be identified at the beginning of a lawsuit with no input from that party, and would receive a notice of potential liability with an invitation to renounce all interest in the patent at that time or else face such potential liability. Later, after the plaintiff loses the case, the third party could be impleaded "after the fact" and made responsible for meeting unsatisfied "loser pays" awards that are premised on litigation conduct over which that third party may have had no control. The required showing of "no substantial interest in the subject matter at issue other than asserting such patent claim in litigation" is not readily intelligible and (just like the parallel definition in S. 1013 in the last Congress) does not clearly limit the provision to litigation that was brought by patent assertion entities, but could capture R&D businesses that have to enforce patents they were not yet able to develop or commercialize.

On the patentee's side, the net result of such joinder provisions would be to create many additional encumbrances especially for smaller R&D businesses, that would make partnering and collaborations, as well as the enforcement of patents, needlessly more expensive and more complicated. Given their potential negative impact on the businesses of legitimate patent-owning innovators, the rationale for creating such new impleader provisions for "interested parties" deserves further debate.

Proponents have described these provisions as safeguards that would only very rarely come into play, under truly egregious circumstances when deliberately under-capitalized paper entities bring frivolous litigation in the knowledge that they would be "judgment proof" against a litigation cost award. And yet, under H.R. 9 for example, a broad class of business partners, licensors, or other affiliates of *any* patent plaintiff would be exposed to preemptive threats of liability in the form of menacing legal notices informing them that they could be joined to a lawsuit over which they may have no control, be subjected to fee awards over which they have no control either, and inviting them to renounce all interest in the patent (and effectively dissolve their business relationship with the plaintiff). And under the process that was proposed in S. 1013, such unwilling "interested parties" would be impleaded *before* it is even known that the patentee lost the case, before it is known that the patentee acted unreasonably and without justification, and before it is known that the patentee cannot or will not reimburse the defendant's litigation costs. But not all patentees lose, not all act unreasonably, and not all are penniless. In such ways, the proposed impleader provisions would not just systematically interfere with the business relationships of patentees of all stripes, but also lead to a great deal of legal conflict over who should be in a patent case at its inception when, after all is said and done, it likely will not have been necessary to do so.[14]

In our view, the joinder provisions under consideration present a great departure from normal civil litigation under the American system, and have the potential for significant negative business impact on investment-intensive innovation, especially for smaller companies and non-profit and academic innovators. The joinder/impleader provisions should, at a minimum, be changed to limit the class of "interested parties" that could be brought into the lawsuit as unwilling co-plaintiffs. Business partners, patent owners, financing companies, and others who engage only in arm's length business with the patentee should not be subjected to potential liability or forced to renounce all of their rights in a patent just to avoid being dragged into litigation between two other parties. On the other hand, with proper safeguards it may be fair to permit impleader of entities that directly benefit from and have the right to control the patentee's litigation conduct. In particular, courts should be encouraged to look to well-established bodies of law that permit vicarious liability or corporate veil-piercing to identify patent enforcers who operate through undercapitalized paper entities, rather than creating broad and vague new categories of potentially impleaded parties.

Deferral of Discovery

H.R. 9, as did bills in the past Congress, contains provisions that would require courts to defer discovery in patent cases except as necessary to judicially construe the meaning and scope of the asserted patent claims. In effect, these provisions would routinely defer merits discovery in virtually all patent cases until after the court issues a claim construction order. While there undoubtedly are cases in which such discovery deferrals are appropriate, doing so as a general rule would effectively bifurcate discovery on the merits in most cases and tend to prolong patent litigation by 12 months, if not longer, across the board. Such delays would accrue even in routine patent litigation that does not involve meritless claims, small businesses defendants, or "patent trolls."

In BIO's view, these proposals are too rigid and interfere unduly with the responsibility and authority of district courts to manage patent litigation in a case-specific manner. In instances where there is ongoing infringement, these provisions would perpetuate uncertainty for patentees whose market share continues to erode, as well as for accused infringers whose potential damages continue to accrue. Settlement negotiations would be hampered by delays in developing a sufficient factual record. The development of other potentially case-dispositive issues would be put on hold, and opportunities for early resolution of the litigation on other grounds would be lost. Interlocutory appeals from claim construction orders would become more common, which would contribute to further piecemeal adjudication and delay. In such ways, legislation that is intended to make patent litigation more streamlined and less costly likely would end up achieving the exact opposite result.

To be sure, the discovery stay provision of H.R. 9 does permit limited flexibilities – for additional discovery "as necessary" to ensure timely resolution of certain litigation that is required by existing federal laws to proceed under defined statutory timelines, or as necessary "to resolve a motion properly raised" prior to claim construction, or to prevent "manifest injustice." But these exceptions do not alter the fact that patent litigation in the overwhelming majority of patent cases would incur significant across-the-board delays and increased expense for all parties. Even in cases where these very limited flexibilities can be invoked, it is clear that litigants would *not* be entitled to discovery as under current practice. Instead, the burden would be on the requesting party to show why its discovery request is necessary and how its rights would be affected if the discovery request were not granted, all of which would be subject to dispute and counterarguments by the opposing party.

If the goal is to address a subset of cases – litigation brought by patent-assertion entities – it is unclear why Congress would insist on such across-the-board rigidity. The majority of patent litigation manifestly does not involve "patent trolls," and while it may be difficult to define "troll" cases *affirmatively* in statutory language, it is not too difficult to identify whole classes of cases that have nothing to do with "patent trolling." H.R. 9 takes one half-step in this direction: as introduced, H.R. 9 provides that its limitation on discovery would not apply to “an action seeking a preliminary injunction to redress harm arising from any allegedly infringing instrumentality that competes with a product sold or offered for sale, or a process used by a party alleging infringement.” Providing such a categorical exemption for cases between manufacturing marketplace competitors is entirely reasonable. It is perplexing, however, that this exemption should be limited only to preliminary injunction cases. Preliminary injunctions are uncommon in cases between manufacturing competitors, and it is not understood how the goal of limiting discovery in patent-assertion-entity cases would in any way be advanced by interfering with patent litigation between marketplace competitors. If there is a reasonable basis for objecting to a general competitive harm exception for cases between practicing patent owners, it has not been articulated.

In the same vein – and of particular relevance to biotechnology companies – patent litigation under the Hatch-Waxman (HWA) or the Biologics Price Competition and Innovation Acts (BPCIA) likewise manifestly does not involve patent-assertion entities. These statutes spell out in detail the identity of the parties, the products that are the subject of the litigation, and the timelines under which the litigation must commence and proceed. Not only is there no question that the parties to this special kind of patent litigation are each involved in the real-life commercialization of valuable therapeutic products, but there is also a real risk that the currently-pending general patent litigation reforms could interfere with the detailed litigation schemes previously established by Congress under the HWA and BPCIA. Patentees under the HWA and BPCIA have very little leeway as to who they can sue, when they can sue, and the timelines under which the litigation must go forward. It would be simply inconsistent with these statutory litigation schemes to now inject systematic discovery stays into these cases, to require the parties to such litigation to make burdensome showings why any given discovery request is necessary under the circumstances of their case, and to narrowly tailor permissible discovery accordingly. Notably, parties to such litigation may not be able to take advantage of a broad competitive harm exemption such as the one discussed above, because under the unique provisions of the HWA and the BPCIA, patent litigation is intended to begin before the allegedly infringing product enters the marketplace. Accordingly, for reasons that are at least as strong as those supporting a general competitive harm exception between actively marketing competitors, a clear exemption for patent litigation under the HWA and BPCIA should also be included in any discovery stay provision.

It also must be understood that not all patent litigation in biotechnology will fall into the above categories. The vast majority of U.S. biotechnology businesses are far from having a product on the market, yet depend critically on the enforceability of their patents to attract funding, to enter into development partnerships, and to advance their technology. A solution must be found for such businesses as well, businesses that are actively trying to develop, and seeking investment to further develop, patent-protected inventions. Any bill that would equate such quintessentially American entrepreneurial companies with patent trolls would be highly objectionable.

To be clear, BIO's members agree that there should not be unfocused discovery during the early phases of patent litigation. Focusing on the *Markman* hearing as the point on which early evidence development should hinge is a reasonable approach, but it is not the only way to address the matter. For example, claim interpretation is not an issue in every patent case,[15] yet every patent case should have focused, rational early development of evidence and legal positions.

Further, our members consistently tell us that a reliable, high-quality judicial claim interpretation is always informed by a range of legal and factual contentions, and backed up by evidence that must have been developed in the case at the time of the claim construction hearing. But it is all but impossible to *prospectively* limit discovery only to what is necessary for claim construction – as H.R. 9 would require – because neither party can predict at the outset the full range of facts and contentions that will turn out to be important for construing the claims. Further, in our experience, it is critically important that a judge construing disputed claims understands how the technology at issue actually works and how it compares to the prior art. And both parties need to understand the other party's legal positions, and the evidence that backs them up, in order to agree which claim terms need to be construed and to put forward a proposed claim construction.[16]

Accordingly, BIO believes that any legislation on discovery in patent cases should explicitly permit the development of a reasonable amount of evidence on both sides, to give the case the contours needed to identify and prioritize the questions that need to be resolved first, be it claim construction or other issues. To this end, it would be beneficial to survey the local patent rules that have been adopted in many United States District Courts, and to explore whether the principles of these rules could be applied to craft a nationally uniform pathway for developing evidence and contentions during the early stages of patent litigation in cases requiring claim construction. Under such a nationally uniform framework, the parties' contentions and supporting documentation, and discovery relating thereto, would form a "default" body of information that would need to be developed initially in patent cases. In this context, we also support the Judicial Conference's recent discovery-related initiative, which would require judges to generally grant discovery only in proportion to the needs of any particular case; and this general proposition would apply in all stages of patent cases as it should in other civil litigation. Such recommended standards, to be developed in conjunction with and implemented by the courts, would go a long way to addressing Congress's concern about discovery abuses by the few, without causing systemic harm to the large majority of legitimate participants in the patent litigation system.

Reform of the PTO Patent Challenge System

The PTO's Post Grant Review (PGR) and Inter Partes Review (IPR) processes, as established by the America Invents Act (AIA), were designed to provide a quicker, cost-effective alternative to litigation. More than 2,500 petitions for such AIA proceedings have been received by the PTO since these proceedings became available in September 2012. The overwhelming majority (up to 80% by some accounts) involve patents that are in concurrent district court litigation, showing that these proceedings are being used in conjunction with, rather than as an alternative to, litigation. This creates a great risk of duplicative proceedings and inconsistent outcomes, as alleged infringers seek to gain advantages or leverage over patent owners that would not exist under district court litigation alone. For example, the way claims are interpreted, the burden of proof, and other procedural protections are less favorable to patent owners in the PTO administrative setting.

In addition, third parties with no commercial interest in the patent or field to which the patent pertains have figured out that they can extort settlements or otherwise gain financially from bringing, or even threatening to bring, patent challenges against critical patents owned or licensed by biotech companies. Biotech companies can be particularly vulnerable to such extortion because – in contrast to most high-tech companies – biotech companies often rely on just a handful of highly valuable patents to protect their products and massive investment therein. This already is being seen by several biotech companies, who have been approached by third parties threatening to file IPRs unless the company makes a substantial payment to them. And a hedge fund manager recently made news by announcing his plans to "short" the stocks of more than a dozen biotech companies and then file IPRs against their most valuable product patents in an attempt to drive down their stock prices. The first such IPR petition, filed by this hedge fund in February against Acorda Therapeutics (a mid-size biotech company which brought to market an innovative treatment for multiple sclerosis) caused the value of the company to drop by over $150 million in one afternoon. A second IPR has now been filed against this same company, and other hedge funds are starting to get into the IPR business as well.

Such abuses of the PTO administrative review system are attractive and growing because, as is quite clear to anyone following the evidence to date, the rules governing these proceedings are unfairly stacked against patent owners in many ways. To address one of the problems with this system, H.R. 9 includes an important provision that would specify that patent claims in AIA proceedings are to be construed as they were or would be in district court, according to their ordinary and customary meaning as understood by one skilled in the art (under a *Phillips v. AWH standard*) – rather than the PTO's current "broadest reasonable construction" standard, which is more likely to result in invalidation of patent claims. This statutory change would harmonize the claim construction standards in PTO litigation with those in district court litigation, thereby increasing predictability and avoiding inconsistencies and wasteful litigation.

An IPR petition filed against BIO member company Allergan on March 9 illustrates that the difference in claim construction standards is not just an academic consideration. In this petition, a recently-formed self-described privately-held investment venture is challenging a patent claim that had previously been litigated and upheld by both the U.S. District Court and the U.S. Court of Appeals for the Federal Circuit. The challenger candidly repeats the legal arguments that had been unsuccessfully made by prior litigants in the Article III courts, but argues that the broader claim construction standard in IPR proceedings should lead to a different outcome. In effect, the petition seeks to leverage the difference in claim construction standards to reverse the results of over four years of litigation in two Article III courts.

In light of such developments, BIO's members have firmly concluded that the harmonization of legal claim interpretation standards between district courts and the PTO is a necessary and common-sense reform that should be part of any final patent reform bill. However, any patent reform bill must go further and provide patent owners with greater procedural protections in IPR as well. First, the PTO has made it effectively impossible for patent owners to amend their claims in AIA proceedings, even though the AIA expressly grants the patent owner this right (as of November 2014, with over 2,300 such proceedings requested and close to 200 completed, the PTO had virtually never approved a claim amendment). Such a rigid approach to the granting of claim amendments undermines the purpose of the proceeding, which is to help improve patent quality and provide freedom to innovate by ensuring that patent claims are not overly broad. Instead, AIA proceedings have become a forum in which patent claims that could be sustained if properly amended are equally thrown out with the unsustainable ones, which contributes to the high "kill" rates that are driving the abusive behaviors described above. Congress should clarify its intent regarding narrowing claim amendments in AIA proceedings, so that they are more liberally allowed by the PTO, within reason.

Second, Congress should include other procedural protections to ensure that patent owners receive adequate due process, including –

- Developing rules for dealing with AIA proceedings that are brought for illegitimate reasons. Most patent challengers who file petitions for AIA proceedings seem to do so to obtain freedom-to-operate, or because they are already involved in an ongoing legal or business dispute involving the challenged patent. But as discussed above there is emerging evidence that AIA proceedings also are being brought or threatened by entities that have no interest in the challenged patent other than to extract a settlement payment or unrelated concessions from the patent owner – or to profit from the declining stock value of companies subject to these challenges. Such "reverse trolling" practices were clearly not intended by the AIA, and they deserve Congress's remedial action.
- Allowing patent owners to submit declarations of scientific experts in order to inform the PTO's decision whether or not to institute an AIA proceeding. Currently, only the patent challenger has this right, making it more likely that review proceedings will be initiated.
- Assigning different administrative panels to (i) the "institution phase" and (ii) the "merits phase" of the AIA proceeding. Currently, before instituting the proceeding, the administrative panel first decides whether there is a "reasonable likelihood" that the challenger will prevail in its challenge (or, in the case of a PGR, whether the patent is "more likely than not" invalid). The administrative panel thus becomes, at a very early point, invested in its finding that there is something seriously wrong with the challenged patent. This affects all

subsequent stages of the proceeding, stacks the decks against the patent owner, and is contrary to basic notions of procedural fairness. It also appears quite clearly contrary to what Congress had intended in the AIA's language.

- Imposing a duty of candor not just on the patent owner, but also on the patent challenger. Currently, patent challengers are under no obligation to disclose information that is favorable to patentability of the challenged claims, but patent owners are under an obligation to disclose all information that is unfavorable to patentability.
- Permitting appeals from IPR and PGR decisions to not only the Court of Appeals for the Federal Circuit (as currently allowed), but also to U.S. District Courts where appropriate. Appeals to district courts have long been an important right in administrative trials in the PTO. This form of appeal helps to ensure proper due process and fairness for patentees in situations in which there is a need for the introduction of evidence that is not available or realistically obtainable during IPR or PGR.

Clarification of Liability for "Divided Infringement" of Process or Method Patents

Incredibly, under current patent law principles, an infringer who arranges for the steps of a patented method to be practiced by different actors escapes all liability because no "single entity" practiced the entire patented method. This legal loophole has existed since 2007, when the U.S. Court of Appeals for the Federal Circuit established a strict rule according to which a process patent cannot be infringed by multiple parties together unless these parties are vicariously liable for each other's actions (e.g., they must be in a master-servant, employer-employee, agent-principal, or legally equivalent contractual relationship). Patent infringers were quick to take advantage of this strict rule, for example by agreeing to infringe the patent through their concerted actions while structuring their legal relationship with each other as an "arms-length" transaction in which neither party has the formal right to direct or control the other, thereby avoiding all liability for patent infringement.

In its July 7, 2014 decision in *Limelight Networks, Inc. v. Akamai Technologies, Inc.,* the Supreme Court (i) rejected the Federal Circuit's subsequent attempt to close this loophole, and (ii) declined to craft an alternative rule that would bring greater clarity to this area of the law. As a result, there is now great uncertainty about the enforceability of process and method patents. Every industrial process that has more than one step is capable of being divided up between multiple actors, and the current state of the law essentially provides a roadmap for patent circumvention whereby there would be no liability at all for, by way of example, a patent infringer who himself practices all but the final step of a patented process and then induces another actor to practice the final step.[17]

In its brief to the Supreme Court in the *Limelight* case, the U.S. Government identified these and other concerns with the law on divided infringement and explained the need for a Congressional (not judicial) solution. This serious anomaly in patent law urgently needs to be addressed, and Congress now has the opportunity to do so.

Proper Codification of "Double Patenting"

H.R. 9 would codify the judicially-created doctrine of "double patenting" for patents that are prosecuted under the AIA's new first-inventor-to-file standard for patentability. While we support these provisions, they do not go far enough. Legislative clarification of the "double patenting" doctrine also is needed for patents that were issued prior to the AIA's effective date.

Patent-eligible Subject Matter under Section 101

Among BIO's members, no area of substantive patent has received more attention over the past several years than the topic of patent-eligible subject matter under section 101 of the Patent Act. The Supreme Court has weighed in on this subject four times in as many years, and patent practitioners are losing count of the numbers of patents that have been rejected by the PTO or struck down in the lower courts on this ground over the past year alone. While in terms of sheer numbers the impact on software-implemented inventions has been particularly harsh, the patentability of biotechnology inventions relating to products and processes derived from natural sources or materials also has been affected significantly by this ongoing judicial and administrative expansion of non-statutory patent law in the United States. BIO's members are greatly concerned by the significant departure from internationally-accepted norms of patentability that is increasingly manifesting itself in the courts and the PTO, particularly with regard to industrial, agricultural, and pharmaceutical preparations of naturally-derived substances, compositions, and processes.

Inventive preparations based on naturally-occurring substances have historically been of great importance in biotechnology, and innovation in this area has been spurred, at least in part, by the availability of patent protection. This is true for every sector of biotechnology. Examples include vaccine preparations, crop protection products, plant biotechnology and breeding processes, industrial enzymes, immunosuppressive drugs, anticancer compounds, and antibiotic medicines. Such historically uncontroversial inventions are now increasingly being rejected in the PTO as unpatentable subject matter under an expanded extra-statutory exception for "natural phenomena," even if they are otherwise novel, unobvious, and useful inventions that, but for the intervention of man, would not have ever been known and put into useful forms to benefit humankind. By subjecting such inventions to an unstable patent-eligibility analysis that focuses on the "gist" of the invention instead of the specific scope of the patent claim itself, courts and the PTO are in the process of creating a deep disparity in substantive patent law whereby whole categories of socially beneficial inventions would face obstacles to patent protection in the United States but remain patentable among its major trading partners, with attendant harmful effects on the flow of investment, trade, and cross-border transfer of innovation.

BIO believes that the Congress should undertake a comprehensive review of Section 101 jurisprudence and PTO implementation to determine what needs to be done to ensure that the patentability of naturally-derived substances, compositions, and processes remains consistent with our nation's best interests.

Diversion of PTO User Fees

On the issue of PTO user fees, BIO's members are incredulous that, after more than a decade of sustained Congressional interest in improving the nation's patent system, resulting in landmark legislation in 2011 and now progressing towards another major bill, the PTO still has neither full funding nor access to all user fees it collects. We would urge Congress to fix this problem once and for all, and applaud Senators Coons, Durbin, and Hirono for including provisions to that effect in the STRONG Patents Act of 2015.

CONCLUSION

I want to thank the Committee for the opportunity to testify today and explain a view of patent litigation reform from the perspective of small, innovative, investment-intensive biotech businesses. I urge the Members of this Committee and the full Senate to ensure that adopted reforms are truly targeted at abusive practices – both by patent owners and against patent owners – and do not have negative, unintended consequences for the vast majority of legitimate patent owners or licensees who simply are seeking to protect and enforce their patents in good faith. The long-term benefit to society of a strong and predictable patent system may hang in the balance.

End Notes

[1] Moving Research from the Bench to the Bedside: Hearings Before the Subcomm. on Health of the House Comm. on Energy and Commerce, 108th Cong., 1st Sess. 47 (2003) (testimony of Phylliss Gardner, M.D) (http://archives.energycommerce.house.gov/reparchives/108/Hearings/07102003hearing990/Gardner1579.htm) ("The biotechnology industry is the most research and development-intensive and capital-focused industry in the world," noting that 98 percent of research and development investment comes from the private sector).

[2] Joseph A. Di Masi and Henry G. Grabowski, The Cost of Biopharmaceutical R and D: Is Biotech Different? Manage. Decis. Econ. 28: 469-479, 2007)(hereafter: "Di Masi and Grabowski").

[3] Secretary of Health and Human Services Tommy G. Thompson, Remarks at the Milken Institute's Global Conference (Apr. 26, 2004), available at www.hhs.gov/news/speech/2004/040426.html.

[4] Di Masi and Grabowski, 472-3.

[5] Benjamin Roin, Unpatentable Drugs and the Standards of Patentability. Texas Law Review, Vol. 87, pp. 503-570, 2009.

[6] Government Accountability Office report 13-465, August 2013, *Assessing Factors That Affect Patent Infringement Litigation Could Help Improve Patent Quality.*

[7] https://lexmachina.com/2014/10/september-2014-new-patent-case-filings-40-september-2013/

[8] https://lexmachina.com/2015/02/patent-case-trends-business-litigation/.

[9] Section 5 of H.R. 9, as recently introduced in the House of Representatives, likewise contains such a "customer suit" provision. Going forward, Congress should consider modifications to this provision to guard against opportunities for misuse and unintended consequences. As written, the provision could unexpectedly benefit accused infringers at every level of the manufacturing and distribution chain, contrary to its declared goal of protecting ends-users and retailers of infringing products. For example, in current form the provision would allow even manufacturers of infringing products to deflect infringement suits towards their parts suppliers, thereby inviting piecemeal adjudication and systematic litigation delays in conventional infringement cases having nothing to do with end users, retailers, or "patent trolls." Additional amendments should provide more clarity around the class of intended

beneficiaries, the scope of the stay, and the circumstances under which a litigation stay would be inappropriate.

[10] In practice, the FEAJA standard may be more often met than one might assume. The Veteran's Administration, for example, estimates that around 45% of all cases before the Court of Veteran's Appeals result in a FEAJA attorney fee and cost award against the Government. Social Security cases in which the claimant prevails result in awards over 40% of the time. The Supreme Court has noted that these are "hardly vanishing odds of success for an attorney deciding whether to take a client's case" (*Astrue v. Ratliff*, 130 S. Ct. 2521 (2010), at n. 2, Sotomayor, J., concurring). It also should be noted that the FEAJA's fee recovery provisions are only available to small entity, nonprofit, or non-wealthy individual claimants, whereas H.R. 9 and S.1013 would let all prevailing parties recover regardless of their wealth. Moreover, the FEAJA caps recoverable attorney fees at a default of $125/hour, whereas neither H.R. 9 nor S.1013 provide such caps – or any other protections – against runaway costs.

[11] To give a simple example: assume a patentee sues a competitor for patent infringement. The competitor alleges that the patent is (i) invalid, (ii) unenforceable, and (iii) not infringed. The court rules *against* the competitor on the question of patent validity and enforceability, but agrees that the patent is not infringed. In this scenario, the competitor ultimately "prevailed" because it escaped liability, but did not "prevail" in its attempt at striking down the patent. Who reimburses whose litigation costs? Does the competitor reimburse the patentee for defending the patent? Or does the patentee pay the competitor for unsuccessfully attacking the patent? Or do both parties reimburse each other for portions of each other's cases?

[12] Synopsis is available at: http://www.insidecounsel.com/2015/02/25/fee-shifting-before-and-after-the-supremecourt-de.

[13] For example, if a complaint were to assert 20 claims in three patents, and the defendant makes the requisite showing with respect to only one of these claims, the whole litigation would become subject to the impleader provision. In other words: defendants would have as many opportunities to invoke the impleader provision as there are asserted claims. This would be the case even if the remaining claims in the litigation involve patent-infringing products that compete with the patentee's own products. We note that the heightened pleading requirements of S. 1013 (as do those of currently-pending H.R. 9) would require patentees to assert greater numbers of patent claims than is required under current law, thereby increasing a defendant's chances to implead additional parties. Moreover, it is not uncommon, especially among start-up businesses, to hold patents on "unfunded" technology. For example, a company may start out with two in-licensed portfolios of patents, and proceed with R&D work on one of them while seeking funding to begin development of the other. If a patent on such unfunded technology is infringed, even a brick-and-mortar research company that sees its chances for future funding evaporate if it does not defend itself against ongoing infringement could be deemed indistinguishable from a patent-assertion-entity under the definition in S. 1013.

[14] If, on the other hand, the reason for impleading "interested parties" is to address "privateering" – a practice whereby large companies reportedly license or assign their patents to other entities that then assert these patents as a proxy for the large company – it is unclear what the impleader provision would accomplish in such instances. For example, it has been said that large companies assert patents through proxies in this way to insulate themselves from counterclaims – but if good grounds for a meritorious counterclaim exist, it should almost certainly be possible to sue such a company separately. At any rate, under U.S. corporate

law, it is perfectly common and permissible to establish corporate affiliates for the purpose of isolating assets or liabilities, and that holds true for IP assets as well. There also is a well-developed body of law that allows veil-piercing, not just to establish liability but also to collect debts and unpaid awards, and U.S. courts have not shied away from allowing recovery against corporate parents or affiliates that sought to hide behind paper entities. We are not convinced that opening the doors to new, relatively unselective impleader authority would accomplish anything that cannot already, under existing law, be done more selectively and with less collateral damage.

[15] For example if the defendant claims that he actually co-owns the patent, or that he is licensed, or that his infringing product is protected by prior user rights, or that the patent is unenforceable due to laches -- for such defenses it ordinarily won't matter very much how the patent claim is interpreted. On the other hand, if anticipation or obviousness is an issue, or infringement is disputed, claim interpretation often matters very much.

[16] For example, if the defendant contends that the patent is invalid in light of prior art, and for lack of enablement – this is something the patentee needs to know with specificity prior to claim construction. Which prior art, and how does it supposedly fall into the claim? And what within the supposed scope of the claim is not enabled? Likewise, if the patent holder alleges, for example, that the accused product infringes the patent under the doctrine of equivalents, then the defendant needs to know which elements of its product are supposed to be covered literally by the claim and which ones are substantial equivalents and why. If such information isn't sufficiently developed and backed up by evidence, neither party could put forward a proposed claim construction.

[17] Those who benefit from this rigid rule have expressed great concern that Sec. 109 of the STRONG Patents Act, which would close this loophole, would create unfair patent infringement liability even in instances where "no one" practices the patent claim. Statements of this kind misrepresent both current law and the STRONG Act's legislative proposal. Patent law has always required that the patent claim, with all its elements and steps, must of course have been practiced, without authority, before there can be infringement liability, and this bedrock requirement would in no way be altered by the STRONG Patents Act. The STRONG Patents Act merely clarifies, in a narrowly targeted manner, that those who orchestrate the infringement of process claims by others do not escape any potential liability. The proposal does not change the demanding showing a plaintiff would otherwise have to make in order to establish indirect infringement, and it has BIO's full support.

In: Patent Litigation Reform
Editor: Richard K. Gutierrez
ISBN: 978-1-63485-526-6

Chapter 7

STATEMENT OF DR. MICHAEL R. CRUM, VICE PRESIDENT FOR ECONOMIC DEVELOPMENT AND BUSINESS ENGAGEMENT, IOWA STATE UNIVERSITY. HEARING ON "THE IMPACT OF ABUSIVE PATENT LITIGATION PRACTICES ON THE AMERICAN ECONOMY"*

Chairman Grassley, Ranking Member Leahy, and Members of the Senate Judiciary Committee, thank you for this opportunity to testify on such an important topic. I am Dr. Michael R. Crum and I serve as Vice President for Economic Development and Business Engagement at Iowa State University. On behalf of Iowa State, I am pleased to offer the following statement, which is endorsed by the six major higher education associations and councils that collectively represent the majority of our nation's research universities, academic health centers, and their associated technology transfer operations and technology transfer officers.[1]

Universities are dependent upon the U.S. patent system and the capacity of that system to protect the legitimate intellectual property rights of individual university inventors and large companies alike. This system drives U.S. innovation and our economic competitiveness in the world. Patents provide

---

* Footnote Citation Information: This is an edited, reformatted and augmented version of a statement presented March 18, 2015 before the Senate Judiciary Committee.

universities with the means to ensure that many discoveries resulting from research are transferred to the private sector where those discoveries can be turned into innovative products and processes that power our economy, create jobs, and improve quality of life.

Universities therefore have a direct, vested interest in maintaining a strong patent system and in protecting that system from abusive practices that can cripple it. Consequently, our nation's academic institutions support multi-pronged efforts to target abusive behaviors, including *but not limited to* balanced patent litigation legislation, such as the STRONG Patents Act of 2015 and the Patent Transparency Improvement Act of 2013 (S. 1720). All such efforts should be carefully calibrated so that they both effectively target abusive patent litigation practices and preserve the ability of patent holders to legitimately protect their inventions through assertion of their patent rights.

The Role of Academic Institutions in the Nation's Innovation System

America's academic institutions are the principal source of basic research that expands the frontiers of knowledge and produces discoveries that enhance our national security, strengthen our economy, improve health, and enrich the lives of our citizens. Each year since the late 1990s, universities have performed between 50% and 60% of U.S. basic research. In 2012, universities performed just over 53 percent of all basic research and almost 20% of applied research conducted in the United States.[2] Academic institutions are also the nation's leading centers for clinical and translational research, food and agricultural research, and cutting-edge engineering and computational science.

University research has greatly strengthened our nation's innovative capacity and economic competitiveness. More than half of U.S. economic growth since World War II has resulted directly from technological innovation, much of which stems from scientific, medical, and engineering research conducted at our universities.[3] Although the primary means by which university research results are disseminated is through training and peer-reviewed publications, conferences, consulting and other forms of open communication, our country increasingly benefits from university technology transfer. Technology transfer is the process by which fundamental discoveries are moved into the commercial sector for development into socially and economically beneficial products and processes.

University technology transfer's contributions to our nation were greatly enhanced by the passage of the Bayh-Dole Act in 1980, which allowed universities to retain the patent and licensing rights to inventions resulting from federally funded research. The enactment of that landmark legislation sparked a dramatic increase in university-to-industry technology transfer:

- In 1980, the year the Bayh-Dole Act was passed, the government held the titles to approximately 28,000 patents, fewer than 5% of which had been licensed for further commercial development by industry. At that time, fewer than 250 patents in total – both federally and non-federally funded – were being issued to U.S. universities annually.
- In 1985, 500 patents were issued to the top 200 research institutions.
- In 2013, U.S. university research led to 5,163 patents in total; 5,790 executed license agreements and options with companies; 747 new companies; and more than 700 new commercial products.
- Between 1996 and 2013, U.S. university licensing activity contributed $181 billion to the U.S. GDP, supporting 1.44 million person years of employment and $404 billion in gross output.4

Federally funded university research has played a critical role in the development of the laser and its myriad applications, microprocessors, magnetic resonance imaging and later MRI applications, the CAT scan and PET/CT scanner, Doppler radar, GPS, bar codes, web browsers, and hundreds of medicines and vaccines, to name just some of the most widely known examples.

Furthermore, university research has not only produced ground-breaking inventions that have led to valuable products, processes, medicines, medical treatments, and new technologies in a wide range of fields, but has also led to the creation of new companies — as noted above, nearly 750 in 2013. The Science Coalition's list of 100 companies that have grown out of federally funded university research includes major companies such as Google, Cisco Systems, Genentech, Sun Microsystems, and Xenogen, a leader in *in vivo* optical imaging.

At my home institution of Iowa State University, for example, technology transfer has led to numerous technologies, products, and processes that have had a major impact locally, nationally, and internationally, including the fax machine; hybrid corn (named in 2015 by the Association of University Technology Managers as one of the forty most important inventions by a university); a method for monitoring the communication signature of digital communication devices that can be used for authentication and other security applications; and a vaccine that can help prevent transmission of the bacteria that cause salmonellosis among chickens and reduce food-borne disease caused by eating contaminated eggs.

Between 2010 and 2014, inclusive, the three State of Iowa Regent universities – the University of Iowa, Iowa State University, and the University of Northern Iowa – were responsible for the execution of 472 licenses and options, including 183 to companies in Iowa. During that same period, Iowa universities generated 1,059 invention disclosures and 767 patent applications.

The Iowa Regent universities also preferentially license the technologies they develop to Iowa companies, such as Iowa Approach, Inc., which licensed intellectual property from the University of Iowa to commercialize a collection of catheter-based tools to treat atrial fibrillation. Over the past twenty years, more than 500 Iowa companies and individuals have licensed patented and non-patented varieties of soybeans from the Iowa State University Research Foundation (ISURF) covering more than 500,000 acres.

In the last five years, faculty and students from the Regent universities in Iowa have launched 190 startups, supported by over $24 million in outside funding. In 2014, Iowa companies earned $24,724,000 in revenue from technologies and inventions created by these three universities.

As noted above, by allowing universities to retain the rights to their inventions arising from federally funded research, Bayh-Dole has created a powerful incentive for academic institutions to pursue the technology transfer that the federal government did not. It is essential to emphasize here, however, that the purpose of university technology transfer – consistent with the overall university mission of education, research, and service – is to enable the commercial sector to generate products and processes that benefit society, *not* to enable the higher education sector to generate revenue. In fact, most university technology transfer operations do not receive enough royalties to offset their total operating costs.

The ability of university technology transfer to achieve its societal benefits is critically dependent on a strong patent system. Because the inventions emerging from university research tend to be early-stage, high-risk inventions, successful university technology transfer transactions must operate within a patent system that protects these inventions. Without such robust patent protections, licensees and venture capitalists will not take on the significant risk associated with investing in and developing such inventions. Strong patents are particularly critical for the small, often undercapitalized startup companies built upon university discoveries. Indeed, patents are often the most critical assets of these startups and small businesses. To be able to gain a foothold in often well-developed markets, such companies must be able to assert their patent rights effectively.

It is also crucially important for universities and their licensees, particularly startups without substantial financial resources, to be protected from potentially crippling abusive patent litigation practices. We also note that many universities own or are affiliated with hospitals and academic health systems that provide lifesaving services to local communities and are often major regional economic drivers. These health centers, too, are targets for abusive patent litigation practices. Accordingly, like so many other innovators in the U.S. economy, academic institutions have a genuine interest in pursuing balanced reforms that address abusive practices and also safeguard the ability of patent holders to enforce their patent rights in good faith.

Balanced Patent Legislation in an Evolving Patent Landscape

We recognize that abusive patent litigation practices are a corrosive assault on the nation's patent system and must be forcefully countered. We also believe strongly, however, that a careful, fact-based cost/benefit evaluation of each of these proposals must be carried out, particularly given that the evidentiary basis for sweeping patent reform has been called sharply into question. Moreover, the patent landscape has shifted considerably since various patent reform proposals were first proposed, creating fundamental questions about the urgency of broad patent reform at this time.

The Necessity of Cost/Benefit Analyses to Preserve Balance in the Patent System

A number of prevailing proposals to curtail abusive patent litigation practices would cause far more damage to the system than the benefits they might provide in stemming or mitigating abuses. In fact, they would have the presumably unintended consequence of eroding the overall strength of the U.S. patent system by weakening the ability of patent holders to legitimately enforce their patents.

Universities are particularly concerned about proposals for presumptive fee-shifting and involuntary joinder. The fee-shifting proposals would require courts to award attorneys' fees and costs to the prevailing party in patent cases, unless the position and conduct of the nonprevailing party was "reasonably justified in law and fact" or "special circumstances" (such as severe economic hardship to the named inventor) would make fee-shifting unjust.

Proposals for waiver of fee-shifting are well-intentioned, insofar as they propose to target fee-shifting at nonprevailing parties whose conduct and position are judged by the court to be unreasonable. But judges already have discretion to make a sensitive, case-specific determination to shift fees to punish parties for bringing frivolous or nuisance patent lawsuits. A codified presumption in favor of fee-shifting would diminish just such judicial discretion and result in increased uncertainty and financial risk that would discourage universities and other patent holders lacking extensive litigation resources from legitimately asserting their patents. This heightened uncertainty and risk also would deter potential licensees and venture capitalists from investing in university patents, reducing the number of research discoveries that advance to the marketplace.

The proposed involuntary joinder provisions would magnify the potentially damaging impact of the proposed fee-shifting provisions. Involuntary joinder would force universities into paying costs and damages for the actions of third parties over which they had no control. As with fee-shifting, the proposed joinder provisions include language calling for courts to implement joinder only in cases where the nonprevailing party's interest in the subject matter of the case is primarily to assert the patent in litigation. The joinder language is sufficiently vague or subjective, however, that a well-financed prevailing party could successfully conflate very different kinds of non-practicing patent-holding entities.

Proposals for heightened pleading, discovery limitations, and increased disclosure would also cause more harm than good. Heightened pleading would add unnecessarily to the burden of filing infringement cases, discovery limitations would preclude cases where broader discovery would lead to more efficient resolution of those cases, and new disclosure requirements would require information that would violate confidentiality agreements, thereby chilling venture capital investments.

Evolving Patent Landscape

Several judicial and administrative actions have occurred since the initial patent litigation reform proposals were advanced in 2013. These actions call for a broad re-evaluation of patent litigation before proceeding with proposals that could do serious damage to the strong U.S. patent system.

The Supreme Court's April 2014 decisions in *Octane Fitness v. Icon Health and Fitness* and *Highmark v. Allcare* significantly expanded the discretion of district courts to award attorney costs and fees and raised the bar to overturning such determinations on appeal. One early study that examined samples of awards before and after *Octane* showed a significant increase in the rate at which awards are granted (from 32% to 45% between 2011 and 2013).[5] A second, more recent study that looked at post-*Octane* grants of motions for attorney fees also determined that there has been a substantial increase in the percentage of motions granted after *Octane*.[6]

The Judicial Conference of the United States has recommended changes to the Federal Rules of Civil Procedure that will make it harder for plaintiffs to pursue frivolous patent claims while protecting the rights of patent holders to enforce their patents. These changes will heighten pleading requirements by eliminating the Form 18 standard, which will make operative the Supreme Court standards established in *Ashcroft v. Iqbal* and *Bell Atlantic Corporation v. Twombly*. These decisions obviate the need for stricter statutory guidelines.

The Judicial Conference recommendations will also streamline discovery by proposing that discovery in patent litigation cases include only documents that are "proportional to the needs of the case," and directing courts to shift discovery expenses to the requesting party if producing the documents would place undue burden on the producing party.

The enactment of the America Invents Act (AIA) provided the U.S. Patent and Trademark Office (USPTO) with enhanced post grant review procedures, substantially improving the pre-AIA *inter partes* reexamination with a new *inter partes* review, and establishing a new post-grant review. Both provisions provide a faster, cheaper alternative to court for challenging weak or overly broad patents, and initial evidence shows that these provisions are proving highly effective in eliminating invalid patent claims.[7]

Scope of the Problem of Abusive Patent Practices

Among the evidence cited for the need for sweeping patent litigation reform is a sharp increase in patent litigation. But the cited increase in patent cases is attributable largely to changes in the joinder provisions of the AIA. A recent study of 2014 litigation trends shows a 23% decrease from 2013 to 2014 to 16,089 cases, the lowest level since 2009.[8]

A widely cited claim that patent trolls cost U.S. businesses $29 billion a year has been vigorously criticized. A recent letter written by forty economists and law professors thoroughly documents the methodological flaws in studies purporting to show that litigation by non-practicing entities (NPEs) is harmful to startup firms, reduces R&D, and reduces venture capital investment. In calling into question the claims made by these studies, the authors of the letter cite conflicting data sources, inaccurate proxies, limited and non-generalizable samples, flawed methods for measuring costs of litigation, and disregard for the AIA and other factors.

CONCLUSION

Abusive patent practices are real and they are harmful. Universities vigorously support efforts to rein in such practices. But we believe that sweeping patent legislative reform is not the right instrument. Such a blunt instrument would do more harm than good by weakening the nation's patent system and, by extension, crippling the innovative capacity of the nation. To quote a March 13, 2015 speech by former USPTO Director David Kappos: "[W]e now have a lot of facts and data showing that our intellectual property system is rapidly returning to health. In fact, I submit to you that there is no patent troll driven crisis facing our nation that needs to be corrected with sweeping new legislation. Of course, the system can be further streamlined to reduce needless litigation, but no major overhaul is needed."

Instead, we believe that an approach involving carefully targeted legislation, developed in the context of the changing landscape created by judicial and administrative actions, can effectively combat abusive patent practices while maintaining the capacity of our robust patent system that supports the innovation and economic competitiveness that serves this nation and its citizens so well. U.S. universities stand ready to work with members of Congress in crafting and supporting such legislation.

End Notes

[1] The Association of American Medical Colleges (AAMC), the Association of American Universities (AAU), the American Council on Education (ACE), the Association of Public and Land-grant Universities (APLU), the Association of University Technology Managers (AUTM), and the Council on Governmental Relations (COGR).

[2] National Science Foundation, National Center for Science and Engineering Statistics, National Patterns of R&D Resources: 2011–12 Data Update (2013). See http://www.nsf.gov/statistics/nsf14304/content.cfm?pub id=4326&id=2.

[3] Robert Solow, Technical Change and the Aggregate Production Function. REVIEW OF ECONOMICS AND STATISTICS 39, no. 3 (1957): 312–20; see also Gordon Reikard, Stimulating Economic Growth Through Technological Advance, AMSTAT NEWS (Mar. 1, 2011), available at http://magazine.amstat.org/blog/2011/03/01/econgrowthmar11/.

[4] See Appendix C of Biotechnology Industry Organization, Measures of Economic Contribution of University/Nonprofit Inventions in the United States: 1996-2013 (March 2015).

[5] Randy Lipsitz, Aaron Frankel, and Hanna Seifert, Recent Supreme Court Decision Takes Us Back to the Future: Attorney Fee Award Rate Increases in Patent Cases, BLOOMBERG BNA PATENT, TRADEMARK and COPYRIGHT LAW DAILY (Jan. 7, 2015), available at http://www.bna.com/recent-supreme-courtn17179921906/.

[6] In the 365 days preceding Octane, district courts granted seven motions for fees filed by defendants and denied forty and they granted eight motions filed by plaintiffs and denied seventeen. In the period after Octane and, as of January 2014, district courts granted 20 motions for fees filed by defendants and denied thirty-three and they granted ten motions for fees filed by plaintiffs and denied two. See Eric C. Cohen, Is There a Need for Patent Reform Legislation? Pre-publication White Paper (March 15, 2015).

[7] According to Kappos, former USPTO Director, 86% of IPR requests are instituted by the PTO and, of those, 77.5% have found at least one claim unpatentable. Id.

In: Patent Litigation Reform
Editor: Richard K. Gutierrez
ISBN: 978-1-63485-526-6

Chapter 8

TESTIMONY OF KRISH GUPTA, SENIOR VICE PRESIDENT AND DEPUTY GENERAL COUNSEL, EMC CORPORATION. HEARING ON "THE IMPACT OF ABUSIVE PATENT LITIGATION PRACTICES ON THE AMERICAN ECONOMY"*

Chairman Grassley, Ranking Member Leahy, and Members of the Committee, my name is Krish Gupta, and I am Senior Vice President and Deputy General Counsel for EMC Corporation (EMC). I appreciate the opportunity to testify on the impact of abusive patent litigation practices on EMC. We applaud the Committee's bipartisan efforts to address this issue and believe strongly that legislative reforms are necessary to protect the patent system and spur innovation and competition.

I am a registered patent attorney with 20 years of experience in patent law. At EMC, I have worldwide responsibility for intellectual property (IP) law and technology licensing matters, including IP policy, patent and trademark prosecution, and IP litigation. I will discuss the importance of patents to EMC, the current state of the patent litigation system, EMC's experience as a target of abusive litigation practices, and the continued and urgent need for patent litigation legislation despite recent Supreme Court decisions and related developments.

---

* This is an edited, reformatted and augmented version of testimony presented March 18, 2015 before the Senate Judiciary Committee.

Abusive litigation has become so prevalent in our current patent system that it threatens to undermine the benefits that the system was created to provide. A legislative solution is necessary to rebalance the patent system and to help ensure it serves its intended purpose: to provide the incentives and protections necessary for innovators to invest in the next new technology that will benefit the American consumer and our economy.

ABOUT EMC

EMC was founded in Newton, Massachusetts, in 1979. Today, EMC is a global leader in enabling businesses and service providers to transform their operations and deliver information technology as a service. Through innovative products and services, EMC accelerates the journey to cloud computing, thereby helping businesses store, manage, protect, and analyze their most valuable asset—information—in a more agile, trusted, and cost-efficient way.

Since 2003, EMC has invested approximately $42 billion in research and development, as well as in acquisition of technologies that have revolutionized the world of information technology. EMC currently has an annual R&D investment of approximately $3 billion, and our investments have enabled us to broaden its product portfolio, enter new market segments, and expand its market opportunity.

Headquartered in Hopkinton, Massachusetts, with additional concentrations of employees in California, North Carolina, Utah, and Washington State, EMC employs approximately 68,000 people in 86 countries around the world. We rank 128th on the Fortune 500, based on 2014 revenues of $24.4 billion.

IMPORTANCE OF PATENTS TO EMC

EMC's position of market leadership is the result of pioneering innovation, hard work, and substantial investment in new technologies. Innovation and intellectual property are our lifeblood, our keys to survival, and our future. We have a 36-year track record of anticipating future needs and building and acquiring technology solutions to solve problems in new and innovative ways.

We at EMC rely greatly on patents to establish and maintain our proprietary rights in our technology and products. EMC and its majority-owned businesses hold more than 5,100 issued U.S. patents. EMC's patent portfolio is regularly recognized as one of the strongest and most impactful in the information technology business. In fact, the Wall Street Journal and the Patent Board recently ranked EMC as the 8th most innovative information technology company based on the quality and quantity of its patents.[1] These patents cover EMC's many innovations, including the hardware and software technologies used in our diverse products and offerings. In short, EMC is an advocate of a strong patent system; however, we want a system that protects and promotes innovation rather than inhibiting it, and we want a system that cannot be exploited by those who would use abusive tactics.

ABUSIVE PATENT LITIGATION IS A SERIOUS PROBLEM

In 2014 alone, more than 5,000 new patent lawsuits were filed.[2] That is nearly twice as many as were filed only four years earlier, when Congress passed the Leahy-Smith America Invents Act (AIA).[3] The number of patent lawsuits filed last year was the third highest ever.[4] After adding in patent disputes filed in administrative agencies, the total number increases to more than 6,600 patent disputes—the second highest level in history.[5]

Some claim that recent Supreme Court decisions, and procedures introduced by the America Invents Act, have led to a decline in the number of new patent suits, thereby eliminating the need for patent litigation reform. We disagree that there has been a lasting decline in new patent suits. We did see a dip in new patent litigation filings in 2014, but recent data suggests that this may have been only a temporary aberration. In fact, February 2015 marked the third month in a row of increased patent litigation filings as compared to the same period a year earlier.[6] Specifically, as compared to the same month the previous year, new patent cases were up by 4% in December 2014;[7] by 36% in January 2015; [8] and by 10% in February 2015.[9] While one should not draw too many conclusions from three months of data, there is significant reason to be skeptical of assertions that recent Supreme Court case law and new Patent Office procedures have fundamentally reduced the number of new patent suits.[10]

In 2011, litigation costs arising from cases filed by so-called "patent assertion entities" (or "PAEs") were estimated at $29 billion in direct out-of-pocket costs.[11] At that time, commentators estimated the total costs, direct and indirect, associated with abusive patent litigation by PAEs at $80 billion per year,[12] and those numbers certainly have gone up since then. Abusive patent litigation is a costly problem that is stifling American innovation and impeding job creation each and every day.

While legitimate patent litigation is a necessary part of a robust patent system, small, medium, and large enterprises are all adversely affected by abusive patent litigation. According to a 2013 survey, startup companies and venture capitalists overwhelmingly believe that the threat of patent litigation has a negative impact on their businesses.[13] Survey respondents cited monetary costs, as well as distraction to management, engineers, and other employees. Respondents also described the human toll that these threats have taken on entrepreneurs, citing not only the impact on morale, but also the overall fear of losing a business. Further, the surveyed venture capitalists stated that if a company had an existing patent litigation threat against it, that fact could potentially be a major deterrent in deciding whether to invest. The survey succinctly summarized the responses on the impact of patent demands on startups: "[w]hen companies spend money protecting their intellectual property position, they are not expanding; and when companies spend time thinking about patent demands, they are not inventing."[14]

Other commentators echo this core conclusion: abusive patent litigation harms innovation.[15] While Congress hears a lot from large companies like EMC, in fact, the biggest impact is on smaller firms, including startup firms.[16] Most of the cases filed by abusive litigants are targeted at companies with revenues of less than $100 million per year,[17] although such litigants do try to target cash-rich entities.[18] A study conducted at the Massachusetts Institute of Technology concluded that frequent litigants caused a decline of $22 billion in venture investing over a five-year period.[19] A Rutgers University study concluded that small companies that were hit with abusive lawsuits significantly decreased their spending on research and development.[20] Likewise, researchers at Harvard University and the University of Texas found a substantial decline in research and development spending following protracted patent litigation initiated by patent assertion entities.[21]

In 2013, litigation by PAEs accounted for 67% of all new patent cases,[22] yet only 20% of issued decisions in the same year involved PAEs.[23] This confirms the belief that defendants targeted by PAEs find it more economical to settle rather than to try to defend themselves in expensive litigation. PAE litigation has cost "tens of billions of dollars per year since 2007," with startups and venture-backed companies being particularly hard-hit.[24]

Especially telling is the fact that "the more R&D a firm performs, the more likely it is to be hit with a patent lawsuit, all else equal."[25]

It is often said that PAEs support small inventors. But small inventors only receive from PAEs about 5% of the proceeds of successful enforcement of the inventors' patents. Lawyers and the PAEs and their investors get the vast majority of the proceeds.[26]

This data does not come from just one or two studies, researchers, or institutions. As reflected in a recent letter to Congress signed by 51 economics and intellectual property scholars, "academic researchers have published over two dozen empirical studies on patent litigation and its economic impacts."[27] The letter explains that "[t]hese studies have been conducted by researchers with diverse views and using different methodologies."[28] According to the studies, "a large and increasing body of evidence indicates that the net effect of patent litigation is to raise the cost of innovation and inhibit technological progress, subverting the very purpose of the patent system."[29] Significantly, "[n]ot one study of the economic impact of current patent litigation concludes that the effects are negligible."[30]

Thus, the evidence is clear: frivolous and abusive patent litigation results in less innovation and less investment in cutting-edge technologies and companies.

We at EMC wholeheartedly agree with these conclusions. While a healthy patent system benefits innovators and the economy, public confidence in our nation's patent system suffers, justifiably, when that system allows low-quality patents to be asserted in litigation and allows abusive litigation practices to be used. Baseless patent litigation distracts innovators, preventing them from spending their time productively contributing to technological progress and to our economy.

The staggering costs of such abusive patent litigation are borne by innovative companies in all industries. While 63% of the patent lawsuits filed last year were in the high-tech field,[31] a recent article suggested that patent assertion entities may soon increase lawsuits targeting biotech and pharmaceutical companies.[32] In short, the patent system that was created to promote innovation, has, in far too many instances, actually had a detrimental impact on innovation by taking money and resources from those who innovate and handing it over to those who do not.

EMC's Experience

EMC is a frequent target of unscrupulous patentees with low-quality patents. Since 2005, EMC has faced dubious patent lawsuits more than thirty five times, and has never been found to have infringed. As a matter of principle, EMC does not settle unmeritorious suits. For us, doing so would be tantamount to giving in to extortion, and only encourage more such suits. Yet defending against abusive litigation has cost us millions of dollars that could have been invested in growing our workforce or furthering innovation. In 2014 alone, EMC spent more than $10 million in defending frivolous patent actions.

Typically, abusive patentees provide very little information about their allegations until months into the case. EMC is forced to devote significant time, resources, and manpower to analyzing vague complaints that are directed at very diverse technology areas and complex systems. This effort is needed because we must speculate about what will be the subject of the plaintiff's infringement argument. And in the process, we waste the time of our engineers—the driving force of our company—studying technical details of features that ultimately are not at issue in the case.

At the beginning of a lawsuit, EMC spends between $100,000 and $150,000 per month in outside legal fees for routine investigation and administration of a patent suit. Once a case becomes more active with discovery, depositions, expert reports, and Markman hearings, the fees typically range from $150,000 to $300,000 per month, and often can be even higher. Added to such costs are expenses for outside vendors, experts, and prior art searching, which may cost several hundred thousand dollars each.

Further, we often challenge the validity of low-quality patents through a Petition for Inter Partes Review (IPR). These petitions—highly beneficial proceedings introduced by the AIA—are filed with the Patent and Appeals Board of the U.S. Patent and Trademark Office, an expert agency that is often better situated to evaluate patent validity than a court. Although EMC is a great proponent of this new proceeding, an IPR can cost between $500,000 and $1,000,000 per patent. In instances in which the district court does not stay its proceedings, this expense may need to be borne simultaneously with the above-described litigation costs.

In total, we can easily spend several million dollars to reach a resolution on the merits of each case. With the expenses associated with such litigation, it is understandable how unscrupulous plaintiffs use the leverage associated with these costs to extort unreasonable settlements from defendants. This tactic is especially effective against startups and small companies that may not have the capital for a robust defense. Indeed, some patentees negotiate scores of cost-of-litigation settlements with the majority of defendants, then simply dismiss the rest rather than proceeding with litigation. Although this tactic demonstrates the frivolous nature of the lawsuit, defendants rarely have any recourse, much less a cost effective one, against patentees who conduct no business aside from filing meritless cases.

Discovery is a major contributor to the overall cost of litigation. Discovery costs in intellectual property cases are almost 62 percent higher than in other cases.[33] In a case brought by a patent assertion entity, these discovery costs are borne almost exclusively by defendants. This sort of plaintiff typically has few documents and fewer employees. No matter how many discovery requests they are served, they can often simply produce all their documents in a single banker's box. There is a significant incentive for a patent assertion entity to drown a large company defendant in discovery requests, seeking to force its engineers, its IT department, and its legal staff to unearth tens of thousands of requested documents. Such discovery costs are particularly troubling because they are unpredictable. Judges across the country, abetted by the lack of uniform national patent rules, have very different views on the proper scope of discovery.

Making matters worse, excessive discovery burdens are unnecessary and unwarranted. According to one estimate, less than one document in ten thousand produced in discovery is actually introduced at trial.[34] Email appears even more rarely.[35] Yet despite the irrelevance of most documents produced in discovery, some plaintiffs still use the threat of exorbitant discovery costs to increase the pressure and incentives to settle.

One of the lawsuits in which EMC is involved provides a compelling example of the need for reform. When this case was first filed, the complaint listed eight patents, with no explanation of which of the hundreds of claims in those patents were allegedly infringed. The complaint generically accused two large EMC product lines of infringing, with no designation of which specific models infringed, and no explanation of why any EMC product supposedly infringed, or which claims might be infringed.

Based on the limited information we had, we at EMC set to work investigating the plaintiff's allegations and preparing our defenses. But six months later, the plaintiff amended its complaint, adding three new patents with dozens of additional claims and a third, separate EMC product line. The plaintiff still failed to identify any specific claims or any specific model numbers. EMC again diligently attempted to investigate the allegations, but the sheer number of claims and the lack of any explanation as to how the claims were allegedly infringed resulted in a monumental task, involving hundreds of hours of potentially unnecessary analysis. It was not until eight months into the litigation that specific claims were identified and claim charts provided.

Then, a year and four months into the lawsuit, the plaintiff again tried to expand the case, asking the Court for permission to add new products and previously undisclosed claims. EMC should not have to litigate for more than a year, investing enormous sums of money for its defense, only to have the case fundamentally change direction again and again.

As a result of all this uncertainty, EMC has spent hundreds of thousands of dollars per month combating allegations that are a fast-moving target. If the plaintiff had identified its theory of the case from day one, we at EMC could have conducted our own investigation into infringement and validity in short order, spending a fraction of the time and expenses that we have been forced to incur. Instead, as is common in abusive patent litigations, the ever-changing allegations make it impossible to efficiently and effectively prepare a defense. This is by design and in the plaintiff's interest, as so many companies would prefer to settle for a fraction of the litigation cost and avoid the aggravation rather than continue to fight on these uneven terms.

Discovery represents a significant part of EMC's overall expenses in this case. The plaintiff has accused EMC products that are complex, refrigerator-sized storage systems that may cost up to $1 million or more. However, the alleged infringement is based solely on a relatively inexpensive commodity chipset that is supplied to us by a third party and embedded within the accused products. The plaintiff's damages contentions ignore this fact, improperly claiming damages based on the entire market value of EMC's products. Despite the narrow scope of the patent, EMC is forced to spend considerable money producing reams of technical and financial information that has nothing to do with the tiny third party chipset that is at the heart of the infringement allegations.

But the money EMC spends in connection with these discovery burdens does not begin to capture the total cost to EMC, which includes the lost time of our engineers, executives, and other valued employees. For example, one of EMC's star engineers was required to formally set aside ten percent of his time for an extended period of time to assist with document collection efforts. This single engineer devoted over one hundred hours of time tracking down relevant documents. Some of the documents were so old and irrelevant to EMC's current business that additional employees needed to be consulted for the sole purpose of determining where this obsolete information resided. And this one engineer was only one of more than 100 employees who were asked to assist and dedicate their time to the process of locating documents.

In short, the system as it exists today is highly skewed. Patentees who file frivolous cases can gain significant unfair leverage by increasing the risk and costs on the part of defendants. They are rarely, if ever, subject to counterclaims, so they share no part of the risk, and little part of the costs. Today, they are rarely held accountable for a defendant's attorneys' fees, even when the litigation they filed lacked any reasonable basis. We urge the Committee to addresses these core issues and ultimately allow for a healthier system.

Recent Supreme Court Cases and Related Developments

Some have suggested that recent decisions by the Supreme Court of the United States reduce the need for Congress to act. While these decisions help bring clarity to, and therefore benefit the patent system, the great majority of small, medium and large entities that have been negatively impacted by abusive patent litigation know that much still needs to be done, and that legislative action is required to address the core aspects of abusive litigation. That is, legislative action is required to secure the patent system so that it operates in the manner in which it was originally intended—to promote innovation. I will summarize the relevant recent cases and explain why Congressional action is sorely needed to promote consistency and predictability.

Limelight

Last June, the Supreme Court decided *Limelight Networks, Inc. v. Akamai Technology,*[36] a case relating to induced infringement of method claims. A method claim is a patent claim that sets forth steps to be performed rather than physical components of a patented machine. In a claim of induced infringement, the defendant is accused of encouraging someone else to infringe a patent. In *Limelight,* the Supreme Court confirmed that there can be no induced infringement unless there is direct infringement. This decision properly returned the law to the way it was before the Federal Circuit's decision in this case, but did not have any additional impact on baseless patent litigation.

Alice

In *Alice Corporation v. CLS Bank*,[37] also decided last June, the Court turned to the category of patents that abusive plaintiffs more often assert in patent litigation: patents on computer-implemented business ideas. The Court held that you cannot get a patent on a fundamental economic practice, like the idea of escrow, even if you limit your patent to escrow performed on a computer. Computers are so ubiquitous, the Court explained, that merely taking a longstanding idea and doing it on a computer is not truly inventive.

While *Alice* is helpful in some cases, it impacts only a small percentage of patents. Even patent cases that do not survive motions to dismiss under *Alice* run up enormous costs for defendants. Plaintiffs who file bad-faith litigation understand these costs, and can still coerce settlements out of defendant operating companies that would rather pay less to settle than to litigate.

Octane/Highmark

Last year, the Court decided two cases addressing when courts can award attorneys' fees to the prevailing party in patent litigation. Currently, Section 285 of the Patent Act says that even when a defendant wins, the defendant still must pay its own attorney's fees unless the defendant demonstrates that the case was "exceptional." In *Octane Fitness v. Icon Health and Fitness*,[38] the Supreme Court interpreted this provision to mean that fees are available in any case that "stands out from others." In *Highmark v. Allcare Health Management System,*[39] the Court held that district courts have great discretion in deciding whether to award fees. EMC filed amicus briefs in these cases urging the Court to make it easier for district courts to award fees, and these cases did loosen the prior standards applicable to deciding motions for fees. Unfortunately, as I will explain, these decisions have been only moderately successful in increasing the success rates of defendants who seek to recover their attorneys' fees when they are faced with baseless patent litigation.

Nautilus

In June of last year, the Court addressed how clear or "definite" patents must be in *Nautilus v. Biosig Instruments.*[40] The Court interpreted language in Section 112 of the Patent Act requiring that a patent "conclude with one more claims particularly pointing out and distinctly claiming the subject matter" of the invention as requiring the patent to provide "reasonable certainty" of what it covers. EMC filed an amicus brief in this case as well, successfully urging the Court to overrule the Federal Circuit's overly-narrow view of when a patent should be held invalid for indefiniteness. Nevertheless, since the

Supreme Court issued this decision, few patent claims have actually been invalidated as a result of the new standard, and the Federal Circuit continues to reverse cases where indefiniteness was found in the district court.[41]

Teva

In its recent decision in *Teva Pharmaceuticals USA v. Sandoz*,[42] the Court took a step backwards in its line of patent decisions, addressing the Federal Circuit's standard review of district court claim construction decisions. The Federal Circuit had always given a fresh look to such decisions, which enabled that court to ensure that a patent had been interpreted consistently across the district courts. But in January, the Supreme Court held that some aspects of a district court's claim construction decision would be reviewed with deference—that is, the Federal Circuit should allow district courts some leeway in interpreting patents, even if they get it wrong.

EMC filed an amicus brief in this case as well, warning that giving deference to a district court's claim construction decision would encourage abusive patent litigation. Patentees typically get to pick the district court in which they bring suit, and so they can shop for the forum most likely to interpret patents overly favorably. The Federal Circuit's fresh review of district court interpretations of a patent had put a small check on such forum shopping. Now unscrupulous patentees have an additional incentive to pick the district court most favorable to them, and that court's claim interpretation will be more insulated from Federal Circuit review.

Twombly, Iqbal, and Form 18

In 2007 and 2009, the Court decided *Bell Atlantic v. Twombly*[43] and *Ashcroft v. Iqbal*[44], a pair of non-patent cases that increased, to a degree, the level of specificity required in a complaint by requiring the complaint to include enough facts to "plausibly" suggest that the plaintiff is entitled to relief.

Today, these cases do not directly apply to patent complaints that assert direct infringement (although they do apply where indirect infringement is alleged) because the Federal Rules of Civil Procedure include a sample form for patent infringement, Form 18, which requires less detail than is required by *Twombly* and *Iqbal.* Thus, today, a plaintiff need not fully identify the accused products; a plaintiff need not identify the asserted claims; and a plaintiff need not explain why it believes that the defendant infringes the asserted patent.

In September, the Judicial Conference of the United States, which is a 26-member committee of judges that suggests changes to the Federal Rules of

Civil Procedure to the Supreme Court, recommended abolishing certain model forms, including Form 18.[45]

The abrogation of Form 18 would be a positive development, as it would lead to courts applying the stricter standard of *Twombly* and *Iqbal* to patent cases. But these cases do not set forth bright-line rules, and inevitably there will be satellite litigation regarding whether or not a particular complaint satisfies the requirements of these cases. Different judges in different districts will come to different conclusions, leading to variable outcomes. Legislation is needed to provide uniform, clear national standards that create balance in the patent system and allow defendants to properly respond to accusations and prepare their case from the outset.

Thoughtful Legislation Is Needed

A healthy and robust patent system promotes innovation and contributes to the continued economic success of our country. Unfortunately, abuses of the system undermine faith in the system and the system itself. Three issues cause most of the burden associated with lawsuits brought by unscrupulous patentees: (1) *vague pleadings*, (2) *excessively broad discovery demands*, and (3) *a lack of financial accountability on the part of losing patentees who bring baseless lawsuits*. We have heard some argue that the recent proposed rule amendments by the Judicial Conference and recent Supreme Court decisions will dramatically change the patent litigation landscape. We strongly disagree. These changes do not fully address the core problems of patent litigation abuse. They do not require a patentee to initially disclose which claims of a patent it is asserting, which of the defendants' products it is accusing, or how the accused products supposedly infringe the patents. They do not reduce the expense and burden of discovery. And they do not make fee-shifting the default rule rather than the exception. Only Congress can effect these changes. And, after over a decade debating this issue while the problem continues to grow, we believe now is the time for you to do so.

I believe each of these issues is effectively addressed in H.R. 9, the Innovation Act of 2015 ("Innovation Act"), which was reintroduced this year and overwhelmingly passed the House by a vote of 325-91 on December 5, 2013. I urge the Senate to enact comparable legislation for the reasons stated below.

Pleading Specificity

Businesses of all sizes, including EMC, benefit from a certain and predictable legal environment. Uniform, clear national standards, such as those included in the Innovation Act, can only be provided by Congress, and are direly needed. Those standards should require a plaintiff to explain why it believes the defendant infringes, so that the defendant can actually investigate the allegations and prepare its case, rather than face ever-shifting theories of infringement.

The Innovation Act recognizes the need to provide uniform pleading requirements for patent infringement cases. The Act would require a patentee to set out in its complaint each asserted claim, each accused product, and an explanation of how each accused product supposedly infringes every asserted claim. This imposes no new burden on good-faith plaintiffs, who are required to have conducted due diligence and arrived at a tenable, good-faith theory of infringement before filing suit. The bill's heightened pleading requirement merely requires plaintiffs to disclose the results of their required analysis. The real impact of this provision would be on those plaintiffs who file meritless, bad-faith lawsuits by making the lack of basis for the lawsuit apparent from the outset.

While several local patent rules require early disclosure of patent infringement contentions, those disclosures are not required until well after the filing of the complaint. These rules do nothing to ensure that plaintiffs have satisfied their pre-suit due diligence requirements. They do nothing to reduce the early burdens on defendants associated with investigating vague allegations of patent infringement. They do nothing to reduce the burdens associated with early discovery regarding the accused products, which is required under some local rules before the plaintiff must serve infringement contentions. And local rules certainly do not promote uniformity, since each of the country's 94 judicial districts has its own set of local rules, not all of which include local patent rules.

Discovery

None of the recent Supreme Court cases or proposed rule changes promises to turn the tide of the abusive discovery tactics that plague the meritless cases EMC faces on a daily basis. As I explained earlier, discovery is a significant weapon used to extort cost-oflitigation settlements in meritless cases. Abusive discovery tactics are particularly effective when used by PAEs because they typically have few employees and few records or documents, and are generally not subject to counter suit.

The Judicial Conference has proposed amendments to the Federal Rules relating to discovery. For example, the Judicial Conference has proposed modifying Rule 26 to require that the proposed discovery be "proportional to the needs of the case." This requirement is a step in the right direction. But when considering what is "proportional to the needs of the case," the proposed amendment requires consideration of the "amount in controversy," a factor that is easily manipulated by plaintiffs. Indeed, in two recent patent cases filed against EMC, patentees have entirely ignored financial documents provided by EMC and instead submitted their own damages calculations that are entirely divorced from economic reality. Patentees would accelerate this trend under the new rule, bootstrapping their own unfounded damages estimates into an argument supporting unbounded, burdensome discovery requests.

Other changes require district court judges to manage discovery disputes earlier, more often, and more actively. These amendments are welcome. But they ultimately do not provide the bright-line guidance to courts needed to make a meaningful difference in the burdens associated with abusive discovery tactics in patent cases. The Judicial Conference's proposed changes will demand more time and attention from already overburdened district courts. The average time from case filing to claim construction decision—a crucial milestone in a patent case—was already nearly two years[46] between 2008 and 2014.[47] The average time to trial was over three years[48] during the same period.[49] Requiring overburdened district judges to spend even more time than they already do on discovery issues will necessarily mean they have less time to spend on substantive issues and will, inevitably, delay resolution of patent cases. Further, more judicial attention to discovery issues may have the opposite of the desired impact, leading the parties to spend more time on discovery disputes with the hope of obtaining favorable pretrial procedural rulings. Thus, asking judges to devote more attention to discovery matters will merely trade one cost (compliance with burdensome discovery requests) for another (costly, repetitive discovery disputes). We need a better solution.

The Innovation Act sensibly limits discovery before the court issues its claim construction ruling to only discovery that relates to claim construction issues. This would help prevent wasted effort by either eliminating the need for further discovery entirely (where, for example, the court's claim construction order effectively resolves the case); or, at minimum, by focusing the parties on truly relevant discovery, that can only be known after the court has told the parties how the claims will be interpreted.

The Innovation Act further ensures that the technical discovery that does take place would be tailored to the issues that actually matter, and that the costs of additional and inefficient "fishing expeditions" would be borne by the party serving the discovery request. By requiring the requesting party to cover the costs of unnecessary discovery, the Innovation Act limits the extent to which those who would abuse the litigation system can use discovery costs as a bargaining chip.

Fee-Shifting

The Supreme Court's decisions in *Highmark* and *Octane* are welcome, but do not go far enough. Fundamental change is needed to stop the onslaught of frivolous patent cases companies have faced in recent years.

In the two years before these cases were decided, motions for fees were fully granted 18 percent of the time and granted in part 20 percent of the time. They were denied in full 62 percent of the time.[50] According to our analysis, in the nine month period after the Supreme Court issued its decisions in *Highmark* and *Octane* (ending in January 2015), the grant rate temporarily increased. In that period, motions for fees were fully granted 32 percent of the time and granted in part 10 percent of the time. The rate of full denials decreased marginally, from 62 percent to 58 percent. Viewed as a whole, more motions for fees have been granted in full and fewer have been granted in part. The number of denials has decreased, but only slightly.

Although at first glance, these statistics suggest that the rate of fully-granted motions for fees has risen after *Highmark* and *Octane,* in reality, that increase is largely isolated to the first three months after the Supreme Court issued its decisions. In those three months, motions for fees were fully granted 40 percent of the time, partially granted 10 percent of the time, and fully denied 50 percent of the time. But in the most recent three months, motions for fees have been fully granted only 24 percent of the time and partially granted 13 percent of the time, with full denials at 63 percent. In other words, in the most recent three months, the rate of full denials of attorneys' fees motions has gone back to where it was before the Supreme Court decided *Highmark* and *Octane.*

As this data suggests, fee-shifting remains the exception rather than the rule. At least one highly experienced and respected district judge has stated that *Octane* does not affect what cases he would consider to be exceptional.[51] Furthermore, the Federal Circuit's recent decision vacating a district court's award of fees to a prevailing defendant introduces uncertainty to this area of jurisprudence.[52] And a judge on the Federal Circuit sitting as a district court judge by designation denied fees even though he found that the plaintiff's case "was certainly a weak one."[53] As we can see, *Highmark* and *Octane* will not provide the sea change needed to effect fundamental reform. Critically, much is left to the discretion of district courts—discretion that is exercised very differently by different judges.

The Innovation Act would level the playing field by requiring, upon motion, that fees be awarded to the prevailing party unless the losing party's position is substantially justified or special circumstances make an award unjust. We believe that this provision embodies the most effective way to discourage the filing of frivolous and abusive suits by imposing financial accountability in the patent system. Simply stated, some patent owners—especially PAEs that are not generally subject to counter suits—have nothing to lose and everything to gain by filing suits, whether they have merit or not. Fee shifting would change that and bring some accountability to the system. Further, it would encourage parties who believe they have been wrongfully accused of infringement to pursue a vigorous defense if they believe they might recover their fees, rather than agree to nuisance settlements to avoid the expense of patent litigation.

The Innovation Act also requires disclosure of the real party in interest and permits joinder of that party. These provisions allow a prevailing party to recover fees, and to file counterclaims, against the entity that is truly behind the lawsuit. PAEs are often shell companies, with another entity providing the financial backing for the case. That entity may receive a "back end" in proceeds of the litigation. It may retain significant control over the PAE. It may be directing the litigation in the background. It may have granted licenses in the past, or committed to license its patents on reasonable and non-discriminatory terms.

This real party in interest should be required to be a party to the litigation. It should be liable for attorneys' fees if it permits a meritless case to go forward. And it should be subject to counterclaims in the event the real party in interest is infringing claims of patents owned by the defendant in the litigation. These changes would give operating companies like EMC more leverage, level the playing field and bring more fairness to suits brought by PAEs and other abusive patentees.

Post-Grant Review Processes

This Committee has debated the merits of reform for well over a decade and has considered all manner of legislation since the introduction of the Patent Reform Act of 2006 by Senators Hatch (R-UT) and Leahy (D-VT). These efforts culminated in the passage of the landmark Leahy-Smith America Invents Act of 2011, which most notably invigorated the post-grant review procedures at the Patent and Trademark Office (PTO). These procedures have proven to be effective and useful reforms for challenging the validity of patent claims and they are helpful tools to eliminate, narrow, and clarify broad, ambiguous patents. These changes were based on the sound recommendations of the National Academy of Sciences to Congress and have been implemented as Congress intended.

In our view, the post-grant procedures have been a phenomenal success. Inter Partes Review (IPR) proceedings, in particular, have been very popular with patent practitioners.

As of mid-February 2015, approximately 2,500 IPR petitions had been filed.[54] EMC has filed 19 petitions requesting the PTO to institute IPR proceedings and has defended 7 IPR petitions against its patents. Based on our experience in these proceedings, as both petitioner and patent owner, we believe the IPR process is operating as Congress intended and has proven to be a powerful and effective tool for culling out bad patents from the system.

Legislative proposals that change the post-grant review processes are premature and untimely. Despite the success of these new proceedings, the PTO is already reviewing and further improving the post-grant processes. According to PTO Director Michelle Lee, the PTO is holding roadshows and seeking public comments and plans to issue interim rules soon that she considers "quick fixes" to the post-grant review process. Additional rules are slated for later this year to address more challenging changes.[55] Director Lee stated, "Let me be clear that the Agency is open to considering changes to ensure the most effective and fair AIA trials possible in compliance with our legislative mandate. We aim to implement final rules by the end of this year."[56] I strongly believe Congress should not interfere with post-grant processes that are working and are in the process of further evaluation and improvement.

I also believe the current broadest reasonable interpretation (BRI) standard is appropriate for post-grant review. The BRI standard appropriately places the burden on the patentee to draft claims that are clearly novel and nonobvious over the prior art. The BRI standard is based on a well-established body of law and has been in effect for nearly a century at the PTO. There is no reason why the standard the patent office uses in IPR proceedings should be any different from the standard it uses in every other patent proceeding, including prosecution, interference, and reexamination.

The BRI standard was also recently affirmed by the Federal Circuit in *In re Cuozzo Speed Technologies, LLC*, holding that "[a]pplying the broadest reasonable interpretation standard reduce[s] the possibility that, after the patent is granted, the claims may be interpreted as giving broader coverage than is justified."[57] We are concerned that rolling back this standard would allow overly broad patents to continue to be used as weapons to abuse the patent litigation system.

Willful Infringement

Patent law has long required that willful infringement only be found where there is clear and convincing evidence that (1) an adjudged infringer took its wrongful actions "despite an objectively high likelihood that its actions constituted infringement of a valid patent," and (2) that the objectively-defined risk was or should have been known to the infringer. This standard is based on a well-developed body of case law that has limited willful infringement and, relatedly, treble damages to only the most egregious of abuses.

I believe legislative proposals that lower the willful infringement standard to establishment by a "preponderance of the evidence" would increase the leverage that abusive litigants currently enjoy in the economics of patent litigation. A finding of willful infringement results in an award of punitive damages. In other civil litigation contexts, an award of punitive damages ordinarily requires proof by clear and convincing evidence. There is no reason to depart from this standard in the context of willful patent infringement. Lowering the standard of proof would lead to an explosion of willful infringement claims and only provide opportunity for further abuse of the patent system. I strongly believe that such a change would be unwarranted and harmful.

Divided Infringement

I also oppose legislation that overturns the Supreme Court's most recent decision in *Limelight Networks, Inc. v. Akamai Technology*. There is no reason to change the long-standing rule that a single defendant must perform or control all of the steps of a method claim for there to be infringement. Overturning the *Limelight* decision would merely belatedly expand the scope of poorly-drafted patent claims. This change would undermine certainty in patent law and upend the well-settled expectations of businesses regarding what does and does not constitute patent infringement.

Conclusion

Congress is uniquely situated to make a real difference in these important areas. While the Supreme Court has been active in correcting some of the flaws in the patent system that frivolous litigants seek to exploit, the judiciary—even at the highest level—cannot bring about the prompt and comprehensive solution that Congress can structure. It takes time for a case to reach the Supreme Court and it only accepts for review a handful of IP cases each term. Congress on the other hand can enact balanced solutions in a single, coordinated approach, such as that set forth in the Innovation Act. The proliferation of abusive patent litigation is the kind of broad problem, causing billions of dollars in misdirected spending, that cries out for a legislative solution.

Legislative action to address patent litigation abuses is necessary to restore confidence and balance in our patent system. The courts have made great strides, but the decisions are not sufficient to address all of the tactics associated with abusive patent litigation, including vague pleadings and discovery misconduct, which force many companies into settlement. The money spent on this frivolous litigation would be better invested in jobs and research and development. I must tell you, unfortunately, that I am certain that unless Congress acts, the problem will continue, unabated. The efforts undertaken by this Committee will be essential to the health of our patent system and the innovation of businesses in the United States.

End Notes

[1] THE PATENT BOARD, http://www.patentboard.com/ (last visited February 9, 2015).

[2] *Unified Patents 2014 Litigation Report*, UNIFIEDPATENTS (January 8, 2015), http://unifiedpatents.com/unified-patents-2014-litigation-report/.

[3] *Id.*

[4] *Id.*

[5] *2014 Patent Dispute Report and Analytics,* UNIFIEDPATENTS (January 26, 2015), http://unifiedpatents.com/2014-patent-dispute-report-and-analytics/.

[6] Daniel Nazer, "Innovation Act Needed More Than Ever As Patent Trolls Roll On," ELECTRONIC FRONTIER FOUNDATION (Feb. 18, 2015), *at* https://www.eff.org/ deeplinks/2015/02/innovation-act-needed-more-everpatent-trolls-roll.

[7] *Patent Case Filings Up 32% in December But Down 18% for 2014*, LEX MACHINA (January 12, 2015), https://lexmachina.com/2015/01/patent-case-filings-28-december-20-2014/.

[8] *January 2015 Patent Dispute Report*, UNIFIEDPATENTS (January 2015), http://unified patents.com/january2015-patent-dispute-report/.

[9] *February 2015 Patent Dispute Report*, UNIFIEDPATENTS (February 2015), http://unifiedpatents.com/february2015-patent-dispute-report/.

[10] *See generally* Nazer, *supra* n.6.

[11] James E. Bessen and Michael J. Meurer, *The Direct Costs from NPE Disputes,* 99 CORNELL L. REV. 387 (2014), *available at* http://ssrn.com/abstract=2091210; *see also Litigations Over Time,* PATENT FREEDOM, https://www.patentfreedom.com/about-npes/litigations/ (last visited February 8, 2015); Robin Feldman, Tom Ewing, and Sara Jeruss, *The AIA 500 Expanded: Effects of Patent Monetization Entities,* UC HASTINGS RESEARCH PAPER NO. 45, April 9, 2013, at 7, http://ssrn.com/abstract=2247195 (patent monetization entities filed 58.7 percent of patent lawsuits in 2012).

[12] James E. Bessen, Jennifer Ford and Michael J. Meurer, *The Private and Social Costs of Patent Trolls*, REGULATION, Winter 2011-2012, at 26.

[13] Robin Feldman, *Patent Demands and Startup Companies: The View from the Venture Capital Community,* UC HASTINGS RESEARCH PAPER NO. 75, October 28, 2013, http://ssrn.com/abstract=2346338.

[14] *Id.*

[15] James Bessen, *The Evidence Is In: Patent Trolls Do Hurt Innovation*, HARV. BUS. REV., July 2014, *available at* https://hbr.org/2014/07/the-evidence-is-in-patent-trolls-do-hurt-innovation.

[16] *Id.*

[17] *Id.*

[18] *See* Lauren Cohen, Umit G. Gurun, and Scott Duke Kominers, *Patent Trolls: Evidence from Targeted Firms* HARVARD BUSINESS SCHOOL FINANCE WORKING PAPER NO. 15-002, August 7, 2014, http://ssrn.com/abstract=2464303, at 2-3.

[19] Catherine Tucker, *The Effect of Patent Litigation and Patent Assertion Entities on Entrepreneurial Activity*, MIT SLOAN SCHOOL WORKING PAPER 5095-14, June 22, 2014, at 31, http://ssrn.com/abstract=2457611.

[20] Roger Smeets, *Does Patent Litigation Reduce Corporate R&D? An Analysis of US Public Firms*, April 28, 2014, http://ssrn.com/abstract=2443048.

[21] Cohen et al., *supra* n.18.

[22] 2014 Patent Litigation Study, PRICE WATERHOUSECOOPERS (July 2014), *at* http://www.pwc.com/enUS/us/forensic-services/publications/assets/2014-patent-litigation-study.pdf; 2013 NPE Litigation Report, RPX (January 2014) at 2, http://www.rpxcorp.com/wpcontent/uploads/2014/01/RPX-2013-NPE-Litigation-Report.pdf.

[23] 2014 Patent Litigation Study, *supra* n.22, at 2.

[24] Letter from 51 Economics and Legal Scholars to United States Congress (March 2, 2015), *available at* http://www.unitedforpatentreform.com/files/ip-scholars--letter-to-congress 1554891030.pdf.

[25] *Id.*

[26] *See* Bessen and Meurer, *supra* n.11, at 4; *see also Patent Trolls: Why No One Likes Them,* THE ECONOMIST (March 3, 2015), *available at* http://www.economist.com/news/business-and-finance/21645604.

[27] Letter from 51 Economics and Legal Scholars to United States Congress, *supra* n.24.

[28] *Id.*

[29] *Id.*

[30] *Id.*

[31] *Unified Patent's 2014 Litigation Report*, UNIFIED PATENTS (January 8, 2015), http://unifiedpatents.com/2015/01/08/unified-patents-2014-litigation-report/.

[32] Robin Feldman and W. Nicholson Price, *Patent Trolling — Why Bio and Pharmaceuticals Are at Risk*, UC HASTINGS RESEARCH PAPER NO. 93. Feb. 14, 2014, http://ssrn.com/abstract=2395987.

[33] Chief Judge Randall B. Rader, *The State of Patent Litigation*, E.D. TEX. JUDICIAL CONFERENCE, Sept. 27, 2011, at 7, *available at* http://patentlyo.com/media/docs/2011/09/raderstateofpatentlit.pdf.

[34] *Id.* at 8.

[35] *Id.*

[36] *Limelight Networks, Inc. v. Akamai Technology,* 134 S.Ct. 2111 (2014).

[37] *Alice Corporation Pty. Ltd. v. CLS Bank Int'l*, 134 S.Ct. 2347 (2014).

[38] *Octane Fitness, LLC v. ICON Health and Fitness, Inc.*, 134 S.Ct. 1749 (2014).

[39] *Highmark, Inc. v. Allcare Health Mgmt. Sys., Inc.*, 134 S.Ct. 1744 (2014).

[40] *Nautilus, Inc. v. Biosig Instruments, Inc.,* 134 S.Ct. 2120 (2014).

[41] *See Eidos Display, LLC v. AU Optronics Corp.*, __ F.3d __, 2015 WL 1035284 (Fed. Cir. March 10, 2015).

[42] *Teva Pharmaceuticals USA, Inc. v. Sandoz Inc.*, No. 13-854 (U.S. Jan. 20, 2015) (slip. op.).

[43] *Bell Atlantic Corp. v.* Twombly, 550 U.S. 544, 127 S.Ct. 1955 (2007).

[44] *Ashcroft v. Iqbal,* 556 U.S. 662, 129 S.Ct. 1937 (2009).

[45] *See Judicial Conference Receives Budget Update, Forwards Rule Package to Supreme Court,* UNITED STATES COURTS, September 16, 2014, http://news.uscourts.gov/judicial-conference-receives-budget-updateforwards-rules-package-supreme-court; Vin Gurrieri, *Judges Vote to Nix Rule Creating Patent Complaint Forms*, IP LAW 360, September 17, 2014, http://www.law360.com/articles/578149/judges-vote-to-nix-rulecreating-patent-complaint-forms.

[46] 712.7 days; or 635.1 days counting only the nine courts with the most active patent dockets.

[47] Year in Review: 2014, PATENT NAVIGATOR (last accessed March 10, 2015) at 21, http://home.docketnavigator.com/year-review/.

[48] 1224.3 days, or 1197.2 days counting only the nine courts with the most active patent dockets.

[49] Year in Review: 2014, *supra* n.47, at 24.

[50] *Docket Navigator Litigation Activity*, https://www.docketnavigator.com/stats (last updated Feb. 5, 2015).

[51] *See* Jess Davis, *Judge Gilstrap Keeps Eastern District's Tight Ship Afloat*, IP LAW 360 (March 6, 2015), http://www.law360.com/ip/articles/628732.

[52] *See Biax Corp. v. Nvidia Corp.,* No. 2013-1649, 2015 WL 755940, at *4 (Fed. Cir. Feb. 24, 2015).

[53] *Stragent LLC v. Intel Corp.*, Civ. No. 6-11-cv-00421, 2014 WL 6756304 (E.D. Tex. Aug. 6, 2014), at *5.

[54] Remarks by Deputy Director Michelle K. Lee at the IPO Education Foundation PTO IPO Day Luncheon, March 10, 2015, *available at* http://www.uspto.gov/about-us/news-updates/remarks-deputy-directormichelle-k-lee-ipo-education-foundation-pto-ipo-day.

[55] *Id.*

[56] *Id.*

[57] *In re Cuozzo Speed Technologies, LLC,* __ F.3d __, No. 2014-1301, 2015 WL 448667, at *6 (Fed. Cir. Feb. 4, 2015) (citations and internal quotation marks omitted).

INDEX

G

H

I

J

L

M

N

O

P

R

S

T

U

V